John Plowman's Talk

Plain Advice for Plain People

Charles Haddon Spurgeon

Anna E. W. Biggar

Ambassador

This Edition
Published by
Christian Focus Publications Ltd.
Geanies House
Fearn, Tain
Ross-shire IV20 1TW
Scotland
and
Ambassador Productions Ltd.
16 Hillview Avenue
Belfast BT5 6JR
ISBN 0 906731 73 9
ISBN 0 907927 23 8
© 1988 Christian Focus Publications Ltd.

Printed and bound in Great Britain by
Cox & Wyman Ltd, Reading

Preface

IN "JOHN PLOUGHMAN'S TALK" I have written for plowmen and common people. Refined taste and dainty words have been discarded for strong proverbial expressions and homely phrases. I have aimed my blows at the vices of the many, and tried to inculcate those moral virtues without which men are degraded. Much that needs to be said to the toiling masses would not well suit the pulpit. These lowly pages may teach thrift and industry all the days of the week, in the cottage and the workshop; and if some learn these lessons I shall not repent the adoption of a rustic style.

Ploughman is a name I may justly claim. Every minister has put his hand to the plow: and it is his business to break up the fallow ground. That I have written in a semi-humorous vein needs no apology, since thereby sound moral teaching has gained a hearing from at least 300,000 persons. There is no particular virtue in being seriously unreadable.

—C. H. SPURGEON

Contents

The Idle	7
Religious Grumblers	15
Appearance	21
Good Nature and Firmness	24
Patience	31
Gossips	35
Opportunities	38
Keeping Your Eyes Open	42
Thoughts About Thought	45
Faults	49
Things Not Worth Trying	52
Debt	56
Home	64
Men Who Are Down	69
Hope	74
Spending	79
A Good Word for Wives	83
Men with Two Faces	90
Hints as to Thriving	95
Tall Talk	102
Things I Would Not Choose	108
Try	112
Monuments	117
Very Ignorant People	121

The Idle

IT IS OF NO MORE USE to give advice to the idle than to pour water into a sieve; and as to improving them, one might as well try to fatten a greyhound. Yet, as the old Book tells us to "cast our bread upon the waters," we will cast a hard crust or two upon these stagnant ponds. There will be this comfort, if lazy fellows grow no better, we shall be none the worse for having warned them. When we sow good sense, the basket gets none the emptier. We have a rough bit of soil to plow when we chide with sluggards, and the crop will be of the smallest. If none but good land were farmed, plowmen would be out of work, so we'll put the plow into the furrow. Idle men are common enough, and grow without planting. The quantity of wit among seven acres of them would never pay for raking: nothing is needed to prove this but their name and their character. If they were not fools they would not be idlers; and though Solomon says, "The sluggard is wiser in his own conceit than seven men that can render a reason," yet in the eyes of every one else his folly is as plain as the sun. If I hit hard it is because I know they can bear it; for if I had them down on the floor of the old barn, I might thresh many a day before I could get them out of the straw. Even the steam thresher could not do it, it would kill them first; for laziness is in some people's bones, and will show itself in their idle flesh, do what you will.

Lazy people ought to have a large looking glass hung

up, where they are bound to see themselves in it. If their eyes are at all like mine, they would never bear to look at themselves long or often. The ugliest sight in the world is one of those thorough-bred loafers, who would hardly hold up his bowl if it were to rain porridge; and for certain would never hold up a bigger dish than he wanted filled for himself. This is the slothful man in the Proverbs, who "hideth his hand in his bosom; it grieveth him to bring it again to his mouth." I say that men like this ought to be served like the drones which the bees drive out of the hives. Every man ought to have patience and pity for poverty; but for laziness, a long whip; or a turn at the treadmill might be better. This would be healthy physic for all sluggards. They were born with silver spoons in their mouths, and like spoons, they will scarce stir their own tea unless somebody lends them a hand. They are, as the old proverb says, "as lazy as Ludham's dog, that leaned his head against the wall to bark"; and, like lazy sheep, it is too much trouble for them to carry their own wool. If they could see themselves, it might by chance do them a world of good. Perhaps it would be too much trouble for them to open their eyes even if the glass were hung for them.

Everything in the world is of some use; but it would puzzle a doctor of divinity, or a philosopher, or the wisest owl in a steeple, to tell the good of idleness. It seems to me to be an ill wind which blows nobody any good—a sort of mud which breeds no eels, a dirty ditch which would not feed a frog. Sift a sluggard grain by grain; you will find him all chaff. I have heard men say, "Better do nothing than do mischief," but I am not even sure of that: that saying glitters, but I do not believe it is gold. I grudge laziness even that pinch of praise. I say it is bad altogether; for look, a man doing mischief is a sparrow

THE IDLE

picking the corn—but a lazy man is a sparrow sitting on a nest full of eggs which will all turn to sparrows before long, and do a world of hurt. Do not tell me, I am sure of it, that the rankest weeds on earth do not grow in the minds of those who are busy at wickedness, but in foul corners of idle men's imaginations, where the devil can hide away unseen like an old serpent as he is. If the evil of doing nothing seems to be less today, you will find it to be greater tomorrow; the devil is putting coals on the fire, and so the fire does not blaze, but, depend upon it, it will be a bigger fire in the end. Idle people need to be their own trumpeters, for no one else can find any good in them to praise. I would sooner see them through a telescope than anything else, for I suppose they would then be a long way off; but the biggest pair of spectacles in the parish could not see anything in them worth talking about. Moles, and rats, and weasels, there is something to be said for, though there is a pretty sight of them nailed up on our old barn. As for the idle—well, they will be of use in the grave, and help to make a full churchyard, but no better song can I sing than this verse, as the parish clerk said, "all of my own composing":

> A good-for-nothing lazy lout,
> Wicked within and ragged without,
> Who can bear to have him about?
> Turn him out! Turn him out!

"As vinegar to the teeth, and as smoke to the eyes," so is the sluggard to every man who is spending his sweat to earn an honest living. These fellows let the grass grow up to their ankles, and stand cumbering the ground, as the Bible says.

A man who wastes his time and his strength in sloth offers himself a target for the devil, who is a wonderfully good rifleman, and will riddle the idler with his shots.

In other words, idle men tempt the devil to tempt them. He who plays when he should work has an evil spirit as his playmate; he who neither works nor plays is a workshop for Satan. If the devil catch a man idle, he will set him to work, find him tools, and before long pay him wages. Is not this where the drunkenness comes from which fills towns and villages with misery? Idleness is the key of beggary, and the root of all evil. Fellows have two stomachs for eating and drinking when they have no stomach for work. That little hole under the nose swallows up in idle hours that money which should put clothes on the children's backs, and bread on the cottage table. We have God's word for it, that "the drunkard and the glutton shall come to poverty"; and to show the connection between them, it is said in the same verse, "and drowsiness shall clothe a man with rags." I know that moss grows on old thatch and that drunken, loose habits grow out of lazy hours. I like leisure when I can get it, but that is quite another thing; that's cheese and the other is chalk: idle folks never know what leisure means. They are always in a hurry and a mess, and by neglecting to work in the proper time, they always have a lot to do. Lolling about hour after hour, with nothing to do, is just making holes in the hedge to let the pigs through. They will come through, and the rooting they will do nobody knows but those who have to look after the garden. The Lord Jesus tells us that when men slept the enemy sowed the tares; and that hits the nail on the head, for it is by the door of sluggishness that evil enters the heart more often than by any other. Our minister used to say, "A sluggard is fine raw material for the devil; he can make anything he likes out of him, from a thief right up to a murderer." I am not the only one that condemns the idle, for once when I was going to give the

THE IDLE

minister a pretty long list of the sins of one of our people that he was asking about, I began with "he's dreadfully lazy." "That's enough," said the aged gentleman; "all sorts of sins are in that one, that's the sign by which to know a full-fledged sinner."

My advice to my boys has been, get out of the sluggard's way, or you may catch his disease, and never get rid of it. Our children have our evil nature, for you can see it growing of itself like weeds in a garden. Who can bring a clean thing out of the unclean? A wild goose never lays a tame egg. Our boys will be off to the green with the ne'er-do-wells unless we make it greener still at home for them, and train them up to hate the company of the slothful. Let them learn to earn a crown while they are young, and grow the roses in their father's garden at home. Bring them up bees and they will not be drones.

There is much talk about bad employers, and I dare say that there is a good deal in it, for there is bad of all sorts now as there always was. I am sure there is plenty of room for complaint against some among the working people too, especially on this matter of slothfulness. When I am set to work with some men, I would as soon drive a team of snails, or go out rabbit hunting with a dead ferret. Why, you might sooner get blood out of a gatepost, or juice out of a cork, than work out of some, and yet they are always talking about their rights. I wish they would give attention to their own wrongs, and not lean on the plow-handles. Lazy lie-a-beds are not working men at all, any more than pigs are bullocks, or thistles are apple trees. All are not working men who call themselves so. I wonder sometimes that some of our employers keep so many cats who catch no mice. I would as soon drop my money down a well as pay some people for pretending to work, and make your flesh crawl to see them all day creeping over a cabbage leaf. Live and let live, say I, but I do not include sluggards in that license. They who will not work, neither let them eat.

Here is the proper place to say that some of the higher classes, so called, set a shamefully bad example in this respect. Our great folks are some of them quite lazy as they are rich, and often more so. The big dormice sleep as long and as sound as the little ones. Many a preacher buys or hires a sermon, so that he may save himself the trouble of thinking. They sneer at the ranters; but there is not a ranter but what would be ashamed to stand up and read somebody else's sermon as if it were his own. Many people have nothing to do but to part their hair in the middle; and many of the grandees have no better work than killing time. Now, they say the higher a monkey climbs, the more his tail is seen; and so, the greater people are, the more their idleness is noticed, and the more they ought to be ashamed. I do not say they ought to plow, but I do say that they ought to do something besides being like the caterpillars on the cabbage, eating up the good things; or like the butterflies, showing themselves off, but making no honey. One cannot be angry with these people, when you think of the stupid rules of fashion which they are forced to heed, and the vanity in which they weary out their days. I would sooner bend my back double with hard work than be a jack-a-dandy, with nothing to do but to look in the glass and see in it a fellow who never put a single potato into the nation's pot, but took a good many out. Let me drop on the hills, worn out like the old brown mare, sooner than eat bread and cheese and never earn it; better die an honorable death than live a good-for-nothing life. Better get into my coffin, than be dead and alive, a man whose life is a blank.

THE IDLE

It is not much ease that lazy people get by all their scheming. They will not mend the thatch, and so they have to build a new cottage; they will not put the horse in the cart, and so have to drag it themselves. If they were wise, they would do their work well, so as to save doing it twice; tug hard while they are in harness, so as to get the work out of the way. My advice is, if you do not like hard work, just pitch into it, and have your turn at rest.

I wish religious people would take this matter under consideration. Some professors are amazingly lazy, and make sad work for the tongues of the wicked. I think a godly plowman ought to be the best man in the field, and let no team beat him. When we are at work, we ought to be at it, and not stop the plow to talk, even though the talk may be about religion; for then we not only rob our employers of our own time, but of the time of his horses too. I used to hear people say, "Never stop the plow to catch a mouse," and it's quite as silly to stop for idle chat. Besides, the man who loiters when the master is away is an eye-server, which, I take it, is the very opposite of a Christian. If some of the members at our meeting were a little more spry with their arms and legs when they are at labor, and a little quieter with their tongues, they would say more than they now do. The world says the greatest rogue is the pious rogue. I'm sorry to say one of the greatest sluggards I know of is a professing man of the "Mr. Talkative" kind. His garden is so overgrown with weeds that I feel often half a mind to weed it for him. If he were a young lad, I would talk to him about it and try to teach him better, but who can be schoolmaster to a child sixty years old? He is a regular thorn to the minister, who is quite grieved, and sometimes says he will go somewhere else because he cannot bear such conduct. I tell him that wherever a man lives he is sure to have one thornbush near his door, and it is a mercy if there are not two. However, I do wish that all Christians would be industrious, for Christianity never was designed to make us idle. Jesus was a great worker, and His disciples must not be afraid of hard work.

As to serving the Lord with cold hearts and drowsy souls, there has been too much of it, and it causes religion to wither. Men ride stags when they hunt for gain, and snails when they are on the road to Heaven. Preachers go on see-sawing, droning, and prosing, and the people begin yawning and folding their arms, and then say that God is withholding the blessing. Every sluggard, when he finds himself enlisted in the ragged regiment, blames his luck. Some churches have learned the same wicked trick. I believe that when Paul plants and Apollos waters, God gives the increase. I have no patience with those who throw the blame on God when it belongs to themselves.

An ant can never make honey if it work its heart out, and I shall never put my thoughts prettily together as some do, book-fashion; but truth is truth, even when dressed in homespun.

Religious Grumblers

WHEN A MAN has a particularly empty head he generally sets himself as a great judge, especially in religion. None so wise as the man who knows nothing. His ignorance is the mother of his impudence, and the nurse of his obstinacy. Though he does not know B from a bull's foot, he settles matters as if all wisdom were at his fingers' ends. Hear him talk after he has been at meeting and heard a sermon, and you will know how to pull a good man to pieces if you never knew it before. He sees faults where there are none; if there be a few things amiss, he makes every mouse into an elephant. Although you might put all his wit into an eggshell, he weighs the sermon in the balances of his conceit with all the airs of a bred-and-born Solomon. If it be up to his standard, he lays on his praise with a trowel; but if it be not to his taste, he growls and barks and snaps at it like a dog at a hedgehog. Wise men in this world are like trees in a hedge, there is only one here and there. When rare men talk together it is good for the ears to hear them; but the bragging wiseacres I am speaking of are vainly puffed up by their fleshly minds, and their quibbling is as senseless as the cackle of geese. Nothing comes out of a sack but what was in it; as their bag is empty they shake nothing but wind out of it. It is very likely that neither ministers nor their sermons are perfect—the best garden may have a few weeds in it, the cleanest corn may have some chaff—but cavilers cavil at anything or nothing, and find fault for the sake of showing off their deep knowledge. Sooner than let their tongues have a holiday, they would complain that the grass is not a nice shade, and say that the sky would have looked neater if it had been whitewashed.

One tribe of these Ishmaelites is made up of highflying ignoramuses who are very mighty about the doctrine of a sermon—here they are as decisive as sledge-hammers and as certain as death. He who knows nothing is confident in everything; hence they are bullheaded beyond measure. Every clock, and even the sundial, must be set according to their watches; and the slightest difference from their opinion proves a man to be wrong at heart. Venture to argue with them, and their little pot boils over in quick style; ask them for reason, and you might as well go to a sand pit for sugar. They have bottled up the sea of truth, and carry it in their waistcoat pockets; they have measured Heaven's line of grace, and have tied a knot in a string at the exact length of electing love. As for the things which angels long to know, they have seen them all as boys see sights in a peepshow at a fair. Having sold their modesty and become wiser than their teachers, they ride a very high horse, and jump over all five-barred gates of Bible texts which teach doctrines contrary to their notions. When this mischief happens to good men, it is a great pity for such sweet pots of ointment to be spoiled by flies, yet one learns to bear with them just as I do with old Violet, for he is a rare horse, though he does set his ears back and throw out his legs at times. But there is a black bragging lot, who are all sting and no honey; all whip and no hay; all grunt and no bacon. These do nothing but rail from morning to night at all who cannot see through their spectacles. If they would but mix up a handful of good living with all

RELIGIOUS GRUMBLERS

their bushels of bounce, it would be more bearable; but no, they don't care for such legality. Men so sound as they are cannot be expected to be good at anything else; they are the heavenly watchdogs to guard the house of the Lord from those thieves and robbers who do not preach sound doctrine. If they do worry the sheep, or steal a rabbit or two on the sly, who would have the heart to blame them? The Lord's *dear* people, as they call themselves, have enough to do to keep their doctrine sound; and if their manners are cracked, who can wonder! No man can see to everything at once. These are the moles that want catching in many of our pastures, not for their own sakes, for there is not a sweet mouthful in them, but for the sake of the meadows which they spoil. I would not find fault with their doctrine, if it were not for their spirit; but vinegar is sweet to it, and crabs are figs in comparison. It must be very high doctrine that is too high for me, but I must have high experience and high practice with it, or it turns my stomach. I have said my say, and must leave the subject, or somebody will ask me, "What have you to do with Bradshaw's windmill?"

Sometimes it is the way the preacher speaks which is hauled over the coals. Here again is a fine field for fault-hunting, for every bean has its black, and every man has his failing. I never knew a good horse which had not some odd habit or other, and I never yet saw a minister worth his salt who had not some oddity: now, these are the bits of cheese which cavilers smell out and nibble at: this man is too slow, and another too fast; the first is too flowery, and the second is too dull. If all God's creatures were judged in this way, we should wring the dove's neck for being too tame, shoot the robins for eating spiders, kill the cows for swinging their tails, and the hens for not giving us milk. When a man wants to beat a dog, he can soon find a stick; and at this rate any fool may have something to say against the best minister. As to a preacher's manner, if there be but plain speaking, none should cavil at it because it wants polish, for if a thing is good and earnestly spoken, it cannot sound much amiss. No man should use bad language in the pulpit—and all language is bad which common people cannot make head or tail of—but godly, sober, decent, plain words none should carp at. A countryman is as warm in corduroy as a king in velvet, and a truth is as comfortable in homely words as in fine speech. As to the way of dishing up the meat, hungry men leave that to the cook, only let the meat be sweet and substantial. If hearers were better, sermons would be better. When men say they cannot hear, I recommend they buy an aid, and remember the old saying, "There's none so deaf as those who will not hear." When young speakers get downhearted because of hard, unkind remarks, I generally tell them of the old man and his boy and his ass, and what came of trying to please everybody. No piper ever suited all ears. Where whims and fancies sit in the seat of judgment, a man's opinion is only so much wind. Take no more notice of it than of the wind whistling through a keyhole.

I have heard men find fault with a discourse for what was not in it. No matter how well the subject in hand was brought out, there was another subject about which nothing was said, and so all was wrong; which is as reasonable as finding fault with my plowing because it does not dibble the holes for the beans, or abusing a good cornfield because there are no turnips in it. Does any man look for every truth in one sermon? As well look for every dish at one meal, and rail at a joint of beef because there are neither bacon, nor veal, nor green peas, nor parsnips on the table. Suppose a sermon is not full of

RELIGIOUS GRUMBLERS

comfort to the saint, yet if it warn the sinner, shall we despise it? A handsaw would be a poor tool to shave with; shall we therefore throw it away? Where is the use of always trying to hunt out faults? I dislike to see a man with a fine nose smelling about for things to rail at like a rat-catcher's dog sniffing at rat holes. By all means let us down with error, root and branch, but do let us save out pruning hooks till there are brambles to chop, and not fall foul of our own mercies.

Judging preachers is a poor trade, for it pays neither party concerned in it. At a plowing match they do give a prize to the best of us; but these judges of preaching are precious slow to give anything even to those of whom they profess to think so much. They pay in praise, but give no pudding. They get the Gospel for nothing, and if they do not grumble, think that they have made an abundant return.

Everybody thinks himself a judge of a sermon. Nine out of ten might as well pretend to weigh the moon. I believe that most people think it an uncommonly easy thing to preach, and that they could do it amazingly well themselves. Every donkey thinks itself worthy to stand with the king's horses. Every girl thinks she could keep house better than her mother; but thoughts are not facts; for the sprat thought itself a herring, but the fisherman knew better. I dare say those who can whistle think that they can plow; but there's more than whistling in a good plowman, and so let me tell you there's more in good preaching than taking a text, and saying, first, second, and third. I try my hand at preaching, and in my poor way I find it not a very easy thing to give the folks something worth hearing. If the fine critics, who reckon us up on their thumbs, would but try their own hands at it, they might be a little quieter. Dogs, however, always will bark, and what is worse, some of them will bite too; but let decent people do all they can, if not to muzzle them, yet to prevent them doing any great mischief. It is a dreadful thing to see a happy family of Christians broken up by talkative fault-finders, and all about nothing, or less than nothing. Small is the edge of the wedge, but when the Devil handles the beetle, churches are soon split to pieces, and men wonder why. The fact is, the worst wheel of the cart creaks most. One fool makes many, and thus many a congregation is set at ears with a good and faithful minister, who would have been a lasting blessing to them if they had not chased away their best friend. Those who are at the bottom of the mischief have generally no part or lot in the matter of true godliness, but like sparrows, fight over corn which is not their own; like jackdaws, pull to pieces what they never helped to build. From mad dogs, and grumbling professors, may we all be delivered, and may we never take complaint from either of them. Fault-finding is dreadfully catching: one dog will set a whole kennel howling, and the wisest course is to keep out of the way of a man who has the complaint called the grumbles. The worst of it is that the foot and mouth disease go together. He who bespatters others generally rolls in the mud himself before long. "The fruit of the Spirit is love," and this is a very different apple from the sour Siberian crab which some people bring forth. Good-by, all ye sons of Grizzle, John Ploughman would sooner pick a bone in peace than fight over an ox roasted whole.

Appearance

A GOOD HORSE cannot be a bad color, and a really good preacher can wear what he likes, and none will care much about it. But though you cannot know wine by the barrel, a good appearance is a letter of recommendation even to a plowman. Wise men neither fall into love nor take a dislike at first sight, but still the first impression is always a great thing even with them. And as to those weaker brethren who are not wise, a good appearance is half the battle. What is a good appearance? Well, it is not being pompous and starchy, and making one's self high and mighty among the people, for proud looks lose hearts, and gentle words win them. It's not wearing fine clothes either, for foppish dress usually means a foul house within, and the doorstep fresh whitened; such dressing tells the world that the outside is the best part. When a man is proud as a peacock, all strut and show, he needs converting himself before he may preach to others. The preacher who measures himself by his looking glass may please a few silly girls, but neither God nor man will long put up with him. The man who owes his greatest to his tailor will find that needle and thread cannot long hold a fool in a pulpit. A gentleman should have more in his pocket than on his back, and a minister should have more in his inner man than on his outer man. I would say to young ministers, do not preach in gloves, for cats in mittens catch no mice. Don't curl and oil your hair like dandies, for nobody cares to hear a peacock's voice. Don't have your own pretty self in your mind at all, or nobody else will mind you. Away with gold rings, and chains, and jewelry; why should the pulpit become a goldsmith's shop? Away with surplices and gowns, and all those nursery doll dresses—men should put away childish things. If some suppose that they get the respect of honest men by their fine ornamental dresses, they are much mistaken, for it is commonly said, "Fine feathers make fine birds." No creature looks more stupid than a dissenting preacher in a gown which is of no manner of use to him. I could laugh when I see our doctors in gowns and bands, puffed out with their silks, and touched up with their little bibs, for they put me so much in mind of the old turkey-cock when his temper is up, and he swells to his biggest. The preacher should endeavor, according to his means, to dress himself respectably; and, as to neatness, he should be without spot, for kings should not have dirty footmen to wait at their table, and they who teach godliness should practice cleanliness. I should like white neckties better *if they were always white,* but dirty brown is neither. Some parsons that I meet with may, perhaps, have very good manners, but they did not happen to have them about them at the time. Like the Dutch captain with his anchors, they had left them at home; this should never be the case, for, if there be a well-behaved man in the parish, it should be the minister. A worn coat is no discredit, but the poorest may be neat, and men should be scholars, rather than teachers, till they are so. You cannot judge a horse by his harness; but a modest, gentlemanly appearance, in which the dress is just such as nobody could make a remark upon, seems to me to be the right sort of thing. This little bit of my mind is meant to warn young striplings who have just started in the ministry. If any of

APPEARANCE

you get cross over it, I shall tell you that sore horses cannot bear to be combed, and "those whom the cap fits must wear it." John Ploughman, you will say, had better mend his own smock, and let the parsons alone; but I take leave to look about me and speak my mind, for a cat may look at a king, and a fool may give wise men good advice. If I speak too plainly, please remember that an old dog cannot alter his way of barking, and he who has long been used to plow a straight furrow is very apt to speak in the same straightforward manner.

Good Nature and Firmness

DO NOT BE ALL SUGAR, or the world will draw you down; but do not be all vinegar, or the world will spit you out. There is a medium in all things, only blockheads go to extremes. We need not be all rock or all sand, all iron or all wax. We should neither fawn upon everybody like silly lapdogs, nor fly at all persons like surly mastiffs. Blacks and whites go together to make up a world, and hence on the point of temper we have all sorts of people to deal with. Some are as easy as an old shoe, but they are hardly ever worth more than the other one of the pair. Others take fire as fast as tinder at the smallest offense, and are as dangerous as gunpowder. To have a fellow going about the farm as cross with everybody as a bear with a sore head, with a temper as sour as verjuice and as sharp as a razor, looking as surly as a butcher's dog, is a great nuisance, and yet there may be some good points about the man, so that he may be a man for all that. But poor soft Tommy, as green as grass, and as ready to bend as a willow, is nobody's money and everybody's scorn. A man must have a backbone, or how is he to hold his head up? But that backbone must bend, or he will knock his brow against the beam.

There is a time to do as others wish, and a time to refuse. We may make ourselves asses, and then everybody will ride us. But, if we would be respected, we must be our own masters, and not let others saddle us as they think fit. If we try to please everybody, we shall be like a toad under a harrow, and never have peace. If we play lackey to all our neighbors, whether good or bad, we shall be thanked by no one, for we shall soon do as much harm as good. He that makes himself a sheep, will find that the wolves are not all dead. He who lies on the ground must expect to be tramped on. He who makes himself a mouse, the cats will eat him. If you let your neighbors put the calf on your shoulder, they will soon clap on the cow. We are to please our neighbor for his good to edification, but this is quite another matter.

There are old foxes whose mouths are always watering for young geese, and if they can get them to do just what they wish, they soon make their market out of them. What a jolly good fellow you will be called if you will make yourself a work-horse for your friends, and what a Benjamin's mess will they soon bring you into! Out of that mess you will have to get all alone, for your old friends will be sure to say to you, "Good-by, basket, I've carried all my apples," or they will give you their good wishes and nothing more. You will find out that fair words will not feed a cat, nor butter your bread, nor fill your pocket. Those who make so very much of you either mean to cheat you, or else are in need of you. When they have sucked the orange they will throw the peel away. Be wise, then, and look before you leap, lest a friend's advice should do you more mischief than an enemy's slander. "The simple believeth every word; but the prudent man looketh well to his going." Go with your neighbor as far as good conscience will go with you, but part company where the shoe of conscience begins to pinch your foot. Begin with your friend as you mean to go on. Let him know very early that you are not a man made of putty, but one who has a judgment of his own, and means to use it. Pull up the moment you find you are out of the road, and take the nearest way back at once. The way to avoid great faults is to beware of small ones, therefore pull up in time if you would not be dragged into the ditch by your friend. Better offend your acquaintance than lose your character and hazard your soul. Do not be ashamed to walk down Turnagain Lane. Never mind being called a turncoat when you turn from bad courses: better to turn in time than to burn in eternity. Do not be persuaded to ruin yourself—it is buying gold too dear to throw oneself away to please company. Put your foot down where you mean to stand, and let no man move you from the right. Learn to say "No," and it will be of more use to you than to be able to read Latin.

A friend to everybody is often a friend to nobody, or in his simplicity he robs his family to help strangers, and becomes brother to a beggar. There is wisdom in generosity, as in everything else, and some need go to school to learn it. A kindhearted soul may be very cruel to his own children, while he takes the bread out of their mouths to give to those who call him a generous fellow, but laugh at his folly. Very often he that his money lends loses both his gold and his friends; he who is surety is never sure. Take John Ploughman's advice, and never be security for more than you are quite willing to lose. Remember the Word of God says: "He that is surety for a stranger shall smart for it: and he that hateth suretyship is sure."

When we are injured, we are bound as Christians to bear it without malice; but we are not to pretend that we do not feel it, for this will but encourage our enemies to kick us again. He who is cheated twice by the same man is half as bad as the rogue. It is very much so in other injuries—unless we claim our rights, we are ourselves to blame if we do not get them. Paul was willing to bear stripes for his Master's sake, but he did not forget to tell the magistrates that he was a Roman. When those gentlemen wished to put him out of prison privately, he said, "Nay, verily, let them come themselves and fetch us out." A Christian is the gentlest of men, but then he is a man. A good many people do not need to be told this, for they are up in a moment if they think anybody is likely to illtreat them. Long before they know whether it is a thief in the farmyard, or the old mare loose, they up with the window, and fire off the old blunderbuss. Dangerous neighbors these; a man might as well make a seat out of a bull's forehead, as expect to find comfort in their neighborhood. Make no friendship with an angry man; and with a furious man thou shalt not go. "He that is slow to wrath is of great understanding; but he that is hasty of spirit exalteth folly." "Seest thou a man that is hasty in his words? There is more hope of a fool than of him."

In my day I have seen a few downright obstinate men, whom neither sense nor reason could alter. There is a queer chap in our village who keeps a bulldog. He tells me that when the creature once gives a bite at anything, he never lets go again, and if you want to get it out of his mouth you must cut his head off. That's the sort of man that has fretted me many a time and almost made me mad. You might sooner argue a pitchfork into a threshing machine, or persuade a brickbat to turn into marble, than get the fellow to hear common sense. Getting spots out of leopards is nothing at all compared with trying to lead a downright obstinate man. Right or wrong, you might as easily make a hill walk to London, as turn him when his mind is made up. When a man is right, this sticking to his text is a grand thing. Our minister says, "It is the stuff that martyrs are made of"; but when an ignorant, wrong-headed fellow gets this hard grit into him, he makes martyrs of those who have to put up with him. Old Master Pighead swore he would drive a nail into an oak board with his fist, and so lamed his hand for life. He could not sell his corn at his own price, and so he let the rats eat up the ricks. You cannot ride by his fields without noticing his obstinacy, for he vows, "Won't have none of these 'ere new-fangled notions," and so he grows the worst crops in the parish. Worst of all, his daughter went among the Methodists, and, in a towering rage, he turned her out of doors; though I believe he is very sorry for it, he will not yield an inch, but vows he will never speak to her so long as he lives. Meanwhile the dear girl is dying through his unkindness. Rash vows are much better broken than kept. He who never changes, never mends; he who never yields, never conquers.

With children you must mix gentleness with firmness; they must not always have their own way, but they must not always be thwarted. Give to a pig when it grunts, and to a child when it cries, and you will have a fine pig and a spoiled child. A man who is learning to play on a trumpet, and a petted child, are two very disagreeable companions as next-door neighbors. Unless we look well to it, our children will be a nuisance to others and a torment to ourselves. "The rod and reproof give wisdom: but a child left to himself bringeth his mother to shame." If we never have headaches through rebuking our little children, we shall have plenty of heartaches when they grow up. Strict truthfulness must rule all our dealings with the young; our yea must be yea, and our nay nay,

GOOD NATURE AND FIRMNESS

and that to the letter and the moment. Never promise a child and then fail to perform, whether you promise him cake or a beating. Be obeyed at all costs—disobedient children are unhappy children; for their own sakes make them mind. If you yield your authority once, you will hardly ever get it again, for he who says A must say B, and so on. We must not provoke our children to anger, lest they be discouraged, but we must rule our household in the fear of the Lord, and in so doing may expect a blessing.

Since John Ploughman has taken to writing, he has had a fine chance of showing his firmness, and his gentleness too. He has received bushels of advice, for which he begs to present his compliments, as the squire's lady says. He does not mind either returning the advice or some of his own instead, by way of showing his gratitude. He is sure it is very kind of so many people to tell him so many different ways in which he might make a stupid of himself. He means to glean as many good hints as he can from the acres of his friends' stubble. While sticking to his own style, because it suits his hand, he will touch himself up a bit if he can. Perhaps if the minister will lend him Cowper or Milton, he may even stick a sprig of poetry into his nosegay, and come out as fine as the flowers in May; but he cannot promise, for the harvest is just on, and reaping leaves is no time for rhyming. The worst of it is, the kind friends who are setting John to rights, contradict one another. One says it's very poor stuff, and all in an assumed name, for the style is not rough enough for a plowman; and another says the matter is very well, but really, the expressions are so coarse, he wonders the editor puts up with it. John means to pay his advisers all the attention which they deserve. As some of the mice have been bold enough to make a nest in the cat's ear, he means to be after them and write a paper upon giving advice gratis, in which they will be likely to get a flea in their ear in return for their instructions.

Patience

PATIENCE IS BETTER THAN WISDOM: an ounce of patience is worth a pound of brains. All men praise patience, but few enough can practice it. It is a medicine which is good for all diseases, and therefore every old woman recommends it: but it is not every garden that grows the herbs to make it with. When one's flesh and bones are full of aches and pains, it is as natural for us to murmur as for a horse to shake his head when the flies tease him, or a wheel to rattle when a spoke is loose. But nature should not be the rule with Christians, or what is their religion worth? If a soldier fights no better than a plowboy, off with his uniform. We expect more fruit from an apple tree than from a thorn, and we have a right to do so. The disciples of a patient Saviour should be patient themselves. Grin and bear it is the old-fashioned advice, but sing and bear it is a great deal better. After all, we get very few cuts of the whip, considering what bad cattle we are. When we do smart a little, it is soon over. Pain past is pleasure, and experience comes by it. We ought not to be afraid of going down into Egypt when we know we shall come out of it with jewels of silver and gold.

Impatient people water their miseries and hoe up their comforts. Sorrows are visitors that come without invitation, but complaining minds send a wagon to bring their troubles home in. Many people are born crying, live complaining, and die disappointed. They chew the bitter pill which they would not even know to be bitter if they had the sense to swallow it whole in a cup of patience. They think every other man's burden to be light, and their own feathers to be heavy as lead. They are badly done by in their own opinion; no one's toes are so often trodden on by the black ox as theirs; the snow falls thickest round their door; the hail rattles hardest on their windows. Yet, if the truth were known, it is their fancy rather than their fate which makes things go so hard with them. Many would be well off if they could but think so. A little sprig of the herb called content put into the poorest soup will make it taste as rich as the Lord Mayor's turtle. John Ploughman grows the plant in his garden, but the late hard winter nipped it terribly, so that he cannot afford to give his neighbors a slip of it. They had better follow Matthew 25:9, and go to those who sell, and buy for themselves. Grace is a good soil to grow it in, but it needs watering from the fountain of mercy.

To be poor is not always pleasant, but worse things than that happen at sea. Small shoes are apt to pinch, but not if you have a small foot. If we have little means it will be well to have little desires. Poverty is no shame, but being discontented is. In some things the poor are better off than the rich, if a poor man has to seek meat for his stomach, he is more likely to get what he is after than the rich man who seeks a stomach for his meat. A poor man's table is soon spread, and his labor spares his buying sauce. The best doctors are Dr. Diet, Dr. Quiet, and Dr. Merryman, and many a godly plowman has all these gentlemen to wait upon him. Plenty makes dainty, but hunger finds no fault with the cook. Hard work brings health, and an ounce of health is worth a sack of diamonds. It is not how much we have, but how much we enjoy, that makes happiness. There is more sweet in

PATIENCE

a spoonful of sugar than in a cask of vinegar. It is not the quantity of our goods, but the blessing of God on what we have that makes us truly rich. The parings of a pippin are better than a whole crab; a dinner of herbs, with peace, is better than a stalled ox and contention therewith. "Better is little with the fear of the Lord than great treasure and trouble therewith." A little wood will heat my little oven, why, then, should I murmur because all the woods are not mine?

When troubles come, it is of no use to fly in the face of God by hard thoughts of providence. That is kicking against the pricks and hurting your feet. The trees bow in the wind, and so must we. Every time the sheep bleats it loses a mouthful, and every time we complain we miss a blessing. Grumbling is a bad trade, and yields no profit, but patience has a golden hand. Our evils will soon be over. After rain comes clear shining; black crows have wings; every winter turns to spring; every night breaks into morning.

If one door should be shut, God will open another; if the peas do not yield well, the beans may: if one hen leaves her eggs, another will bring out all her brood: there's a bright side to all things, and a good God everywhere. Somewhere or other in the worst flood of trouble there always is a dry spot for contentment to get its foot on. If there were not it would learn to swim.

Friends, let us take to patience and water gruel, as the old folks used to tell us, rather than catch the miserables, and give others the disease by wickedly finding fault with God. The best remedy for affliction is submitting to providence. What cannot be cured must be endured. If we cannot get bacon, let us bless God that there are still some cabbages in the garden. Must is a hard nut to crack, but it has a sweet kernel. "All things work together for good to them that love God." Whatever falls from the skies is, sooner or later, good for the land: whatever comes to us from God is worth having, even though it be a rod. We cannot by nature like trouble any more than a mouse can fall in love with a cat. Paul by grace came to glory in tribulations also. Losses and crosses are heavy to bear, but when our hearts are right with God it is wonderful how easy the yoke becomes. We must needs go to glory by the way of weeping cross; and as we were never promised that we should ride to Heaven in a feather bed, we must not be disappointed when we see the road to be rough, as our fathers found before us. All's well that ends well; and, therefore, let us plow the heaviest soil with our eye on the sheaves of harvest, and learn to sing at our labor while others murmur.

Gossips

IN WALTON CHURCH, in our county, there is a brank, or scold's bridle, which was used in years gone by to keep women's tongues from troubling their husbands and their neighbors. They did queer things in those good old times. Was this bridle a proof of what our parson calls the wisdom of our ancestors, or was it a bit of needless cruelty?

"It is nothing—only a woman drowning," is a wicked and spiteful old saying, which, like the bridle, came out of the common notion that women do a world of mischief with their tongues. Is it so or not? John Ploughman will leave somebody else to answer, for he owns that he cannot keep a secret himself. He likes a dish of chat as well as anybody; only John does not care for cracking people's characters, and hates the slander which is so sweet to some people's teeth. John puts the question to wiser men than himself: Are women much worse than men in this business? They say that silence is a fine jewel for a woman, but it is very little worn. Is it so? Is it true that a woman only conceals what she does not know? Are women's tongues like lambs' tails, always wagging? They say foxes are all tail, and women all tongue. Is this false or not? Was that old prayer a needful one—"From big guns and women's tongues deliver us"? John has a good and quiet wife of his own, whose voice is so sweet that he cannot hear it too often, and therefore he is not a fair judge; but he is half afraid that some other women would sooner preach than pray, and would not require strong tea to set their clappers going. Still what is sauce for the goose is sauce for the gander, and some men are quite as bad blabs as the women.

What a pity that there is not a tax upon words: what an income would come from it; but, alas, talking pays no toll! And if lies paid double, the government might pay off the national debt; but who could collect the money? Common fame is a common liar. Hearsay is half lies. A tale never loses in the telling. As a snowball grows by rolling, so does a story. They who talk much lie much. If men only said what was true, what a peaceable world we should see! Silence seldom makes mischief; but talking is a plague to the parish. Silence is wisdom. By this rule, wise men and wise women are scarce. Still waters are the deepest; but the shallowest brooks brawl the most; this shows how plentiful fools must be. An open mouth shows an empty head. If the chest had gold or silver in it, it would not always stand open. Talking comes by nature, but it needs a good deal of training to learn to be quiet; yet regard for truth should put a bit into every honest man's mouth, and a bridle upon every good woman's tongue.

If we must talk, at least let us be free from slander, but let us not blister our tongues with backbiting. Slander may be sport to talebearers, but it is death to those whom they abuse. We can commit murder with the tongue as well as with the hand. The worst evil you can do a man is to injure his character. The Quaker said to his dog, "I'll not beat thee, nor abuse thee, but I'll give thee an ill name." All are not thieves that dogs bark at, but they are generally treated as if they were. The world for the most part believe that where there is smoke there is fire, and what everybody says must be true. Let us then be careful that we do not hurt our neighbor in so tender a point as his character, for it is hard to get dirt off if it is once thrown on; and when a man is once in people's bad books, he is hardly ever quite out of them. If we would be sure not to speak amiss, it might be as well to speak as little as possible. If all men's sins were divided into two bundles, half of them would be sins of the tongue. "If any man offend not in word, the same is a perfect man, and able also to bridle the whole body."

Gossips of both genders, give up the shameful trade of talebearing; don't be the Devil's bellows to blow up the fire of strife. Leave off setting people by the ears. If you do not cut a bit off your tongues, at least season them with the salt of grace. Praise God more and blame neighbors less. Any goose can cackle, any fly can find out a sore place, any empty barrel can give forth sound, any brier can tear a man's flesh. No flies will go down your throat if you keep your mouth shut, and no evil speaking will come up. Think much, but say little. Be quick at work and slow at talk; above all, ask the Lord to set a watch over your lips.

Opportunities

SOME MEN ARE NEVER AWAKE when the train starts, but crawl into the station just in time to see that everybody is gone, and then sleepily say, "Dear me, is the train gone? My watch must have stopped in the night!" They always come into town a day after the fair, and open their wares an hour after the market is over. They make their hay when the sun has left off shining, and cut their corn as soon as the fine weather is ended. They cry, "Hold hard!" after the shot has left the gun, and lock the stable door when the steed is stolen. They are like a cow's tail, always behind; they take time by the heels, and not by the forelock, if indeed they ever take him at all. They are no more worth than an old almanac; their time has gone for being of use; but, unfortunately, you cannot throw them away as you would the almanac, for they are like the cross old lady who had an annuity left her, and meant to take out the full value of it; they won't die, though they are of no use alive. Take-it-easy and Live-long are first cousins, they say, and the more's the pity. If they are immortal till their work is done, they will not die in a hurry, for they have not even begun to work. Shiftless people generally excuse their laziness by saying, "They are only a little behind"; but a little too late is much too late, and a miss is as good as a mile. My neighbor Sykes covered up his well after his child was drowned in it, and was very busy down at the Old Farm bringing up buckets of water after every stick of the

OPPORTUNITIES

house had been burned; one of these days he will be for making his will when he can't hold a pen, and he will be trying to repent of his sins when his senses are going.

These slow coaches think that tomorrow is better than today, and take for their rule an old proverb turned topsy-turvy—"Never do today what you can put off till tomorrow." They are forever waiting until their ship comes home; always dreaming about things looking up by-and-by; while grass grows in their furrows, and the cows get through the gaps in their hedges. If the birds would but wait to have salt put on their tails, what a breakfast they would take home to their families! But while things move as fast as they do, the youngsters at home will have to fill their mouths with empty spoons. "Never mind," say they, "there are better times coming, wait a little longer." Their birds are all in the bush, and rare fat ones they are, according to their account. So they had need to be, for they have had none in the hand yet, and wife and children are half starved. Something will turn up, they say; why don't the stupids go and turn it up themselves? Time and tide wait for no man, and yet these fellows loiter about as if they had a freehold of time, a lease on their lives, and a rabbit warren of opportunities. They will find out their mistake when want finds *them* out, and that will not be long with some in our village, for they are already a long way on the road to Needham. They who would not plow must not expect to eat; they who waste the spring will have a lean autumn. They would not strike when the iron was hot, and they will soon find the cold iron very hard.

> He that will not when he may,
> When he will he shall have nay.

Time is not tied to a post, like a horse to a manger; it passes like the wind, and he who would grind his corn by it must set the mill-sails. He that gapes till he be fed, will gape till he be dead. Nothing is to be got without pains except poverty and dirt. In the old days they said, "Jack gets on by his stupidity." Jack would find it very different nowadays, I think; but never in old times, or any other times, would Jack get on by foolishly letting present chances slip by him; for hares never run into the mouths of sleeping dogs. He that hath time, and looks for better time, time comes that he repents himself of time. There's no good in lying down and crying, "God help us!" God helps those who help themselves. When I see a man who declares that the times are bad, and that he is always unlucky, I generally say to myself, that old goose did not sit on the eggs till they were all addled. Now providence is to be blamed because they won't hatch. I never had any faith in luck at all, except that I believe good luck will carry a man over a ditch if he jumps well, and will put a bit of bacon into his pot if he looks after his garden and keeps a pig. Luck generally comes to those who look after it, and my notion is that it taps at least once in a lifetime at everybody's door. If industry does not open it, away it goes. Those who have lost the last coach, and let every opportunity slip by them, turn to abusing providence for setting everything against them. "If I were a hatter," says one, "men would be born without heads." "If I went to the sea for water," quotes another, "I should find it dried up." Every wind is foul for a crazy ship. Neither the wise nor the wealthy can help him who has long refused to help himself.

John Ploughman in the most genteel manner sends his compliments to his friends, and now that harvest is over, and the hops all picked, according to promise, he intends giving them a bit of poetry, just to show that he is trying the polishing brushes. John asked the minister to lend him one of the poets, and he gave him the works of George Herbert—very good, no doubt, but rather tangled, like Harkaway Wood. Still, there's a good deal in the queer old verses, and every now and then one comes upon clusters of the sweetest nuts, but some of them are rather hard to crack. The following verse is somewhat near the subject now in hand, and is plain enough in *reason,* though, begging the poet's pardon, John can't see a *rhyme* in it; however, as it is by the great Herbert, it must be good, and will do well enough to ornament John's talk, like a flower stuck in a buttonhole of his Sunday coat.

> Let thy mind still be bent, still plotting where,
> And when, and how thy business may be done.
> Slackness breeds worms; but the sure traveller,
> Though he alight sometimes, still goeth on.
> Acting and stirring spirits live alone:
> Write on the others, *Here lies such a one.*

Keep Your Eyes Open

To get through this world a man must look about him, and even sleep with one eye open. There are many baits for fishes, many nets for birds, and many traps for men. While foxes are so common we must not be geese. There is a very great difference in this matter among people of my acquaintance: many see more with one eye than others with two, and many have fine eyes and cannot see a jot. All heads are not sense-boxes. Some are so cunning that they suspect everybody, and so live all their lives in miserable fear of their neighbors. Others are so simple that every knave takes them in, and makes his penny of them. One man tries to see through a brick wall, and hurts his eyes; another finds out a hole in it, and sees as far as he pleases. Some work at the mouth of a furnace, and are never scorched; others burn their hands at the fire when they only mean to warm them. It is true that no one can give another experience, and we must all pick up wit for ourselves; yet I shall venture to give some of the homely cautions which have served my turn, and perhaps they may be of use to others.

Nobody is more like an honest man than a thorough rogue. When you see a man with a great deal of religion displayed in his shop window, you may depend upon it he keeps a very small stock of it within. Do not choose your friend by his looks. Handsome shoes often pinch the feet. Don't be fond of compliments. Remember, "Thank you, pussy, and thank you, pussy," killed the cat. Don't believe in the man who talks most; for mewing cats are very seldom good mousers. By no means put yourself in another person's power. If you put your thumb between two grinders, they are very apt to bite. Drink nothing without seeing it; sign nothing without reading it, and make sure that it means no more than it says. Don't go to law unless you have nothing to lose: lawyers' houses are built on fools' heads. In any business, never wade into water where you cannot see the bottom. Put no dependence upon the label of a bag, and count money after your own kin. See the sack opened before you buy what is in it; for he who trades in the dark asks to be cheated. Keep clear of the man who does not value his own character. Beware of everyone who swears. He who would blaspheme his Maker would make no bones of lying or stealing. Beware of no man more than of yourself. We carry our worst enemies within us. When a new opinion or doctrine comes before you, do not bite till you know whether it is bread or a stone; do not be sure that the gingerbread is good because of the gilt on it. Never shout hello till you are quite out of the wood; don't cry fried fish till they are caught in the net. There's always time enough to boast—wait a little longer. Don't throw away dirty water till you have got clean. Keep on at scraping the roads till you can get better work; for the poorest pay is better than none, and the humblest office is better than being out of employment. Always give up the road to bulls and madmen. Never fight with a coalheaver or contend with a base character; they will be sure to blacken you.

> Neither trust nor contend,
> Nor lay wagers, nor lend,
> And you may depend
> You'll have peace to your end.

I cannot say quite so much as that old rhyme does, for there's more than that wanted to give peace, but certainly it will help to it. Never ride a broken-kneed horse. The trader who has once been a fraudulent bankrupt is not the man for you to deal with. A rickety chair is a dangerous seat. Be shy of people who are over polite; don't be too fast with those who are forward and rough. When you suspect a design in anything, be on your guard. Set the trap as soon as you smell a rat, but mind you don't catch your own fingers in it. Have very little to do with a boaster, and though he brags that all his goods, and even his copper kettles, are gold and silver, you will soon find out that a boaster and a liar are first cousins. Commit all your secrets to no man. Trust in God with all your heart, but let your confidence in friends be weighed in the balances of prudence, seeing that men are but men, and all men are frail. Trust not great weights to slender threads, yet be not evermore suspicious, for suspicion is a cowardly virtue at best. Men are not angels, remember that; but they are not devils, and it is too bad to think them so. Our governors imprison gipsies for telling fortunes, yet they give fat livings to those vagabonds who deceive the people in much weightier things. Lastly, my advice to all is—remember that good wisdom is that which will turn out to be wise in the end. Seek it, friends, and seek it at the hands of the wisest of all teachers, the Lord Jesus. Trust Him, and He will never fail you; be guided by His Word, and it will never mislead you; pray in His name, and your requests shall be granted. Remember, he that leans on man will find him a broken reed, but he who builds on Christ has a firm foundation. You may follow Jesus with your eyes shut if you please. When others would guide you keep all your eyes open even if you have a dozen, and all of them as powerful as telescopes.

Thoughts About Thought

THIS PAPER is very little of it to be set down to the account of John Ploughman, for our minister, as I may say, found the horses and held the plow handles, and the plowman only put in a smack of the whip every now and then, just to keep folks awake. "Two heads are better than one," said the woman when she took her dog with her to market: begging his pardon, our minister is the woman, and the only sensible head in the whole affair. He is a man who is used to giving his people many things of a very different sort from anything which a plowman is likely to turn out of his wallet. I have, at his request, dropped in a few homely proverbs into his thoughts, as he says, "by way of salt"; which is his very kind way of putting it. I only hope I have not spoiled his writing with my rough expressions. If he thinks well of it, I should like a few more of his pieces to tack my sayings to. The public shall always be honestly told whether the remarks are to be considered as "John Ploughman's Talk," or as the writings of two characters rolled into one.

There are not so many hours in a year as there may be thoughts in an hour. Thoughts fly in flocks, like starlings, and swarm like bees. Like the leaves in autumn, there is no counting them; like links in a chain, one draws on another. What a restless being man is! His thoughts dance up and down like midges in a summer's evening. Like a clock full of wheels, with the pendulum in full swing, his mind moves as fast as time flies. This makes thinking such an important business. Many littles make much; so many light thoughts make a great weight of sin. A grain of sand is light enough, but Solomon tells us that a heap of sand is heavy. Where there are so many children the mother had need look well after them. We ought to mind our thoughts. If they turn to be our enemies, they will be too many for us, and will drag us down to ruin. Thoughts from Heaven, like birds in spring, will fill our souls with music; but thoughts of evil will sting us like vipers.

There is a notion abroad that thought is free; but I remember reading, that although thoughts are toll-free, they are not Hell-free. That saying quite agrees with the good old Book. We cannot be summoned before an earthly court for thinking; but depend upon it we shall have to be tried for it at the Last Assizes. Evil thoughts are the marrow of sin; the malt that sin is brewed from; the tinder which catches the sparks of the devil's temptations! the churn in which the milk of imagination is churned into purpose and plan; the nest in which all evil birds lay their eggs. As sure as fire burns brushwood as well as logs, God will punish thoughts of sin as well as deeds of sin.

Let no one suppose that thoughts are not known to the Lord. He has a window into the closest closet of the soul; a window to which there are no shutters. As we watch bees in a glass hive, so does the eye of the Lord see us. The Bible says, "Hell and destruction are before the Lord: how much more then the hearts of the children of men?" Man is all outside to God. With Heaven there are no secrets. That which is done in the private chamber of the heart is as public as the streets before the all-seeing eye.

THOUGHTS ABOUT THOUGHT

Some will say that they cannot help having bad thoughts; that may be, but the question is, do they hate them or not? We cannot keep thieves from looking in at our windows, but if we open our doors to them, and receive them joyfully, we are as bad as they. We cannot help the birds flying over our heads; but we may keep them from building their nests in our hair. Vain thoughts will knock at the door, but we must not open to them. Though sinful thoughts *rise,* they must not *reign*. He who turns a morsel over and over in his mouth, does so because he likes the flavor. He who meditates upon evil, loves it, and is ripe to commit it. Think of the Devil, and he will appear; turn your thoughts toward sin, and your hands will soon follow. Snails leave their slime behind them, and so do vain thoughts. An arrow may fly through the air, and leave no trace; but an ill thought always leaves a trail like a serpent. Where there is much traffic of bad thinking, there will be much mire and dirt. Every wave of wicked thought adds something to the corruption which rots upon the shore of life. It is dreadful to think, that a vile imagination, once indulged, gets the key of our minds, and can get in again very easily. Whether we will or no, it can so return as to bring seven other spirits with it more wicked than itself; and what may follow, no one knows. Nurse sin on the knees of thought, and it will grow into a giant. Dip tow in naphtha, and how it will blaze when fire gets to it! Lay a man asoak in depraved thought, and he is ready to flame up into open sin as soon as ever opportunity occurs. This shows us the wisdom of watching, every day, the thoughts and imaginations of our hearts. Good thoughts are blessed guests, and should be heartily welcomed, well fed, and much sought after. Like rose leaves, they give out a sweet smell if laid up in the jar of memory. They cannot be too much cultivated;

they are a crop which enriches the soil. As the hen broods her chickens under her wings, so should we cherish all holy thoughts. As the poor man's ewe lamb ate of his own bread and lay in his bosom, even so should godly meditation be very dear to us. Holy thoughts breed holy words and holy actions, and are hopeful evidences of a renewed heart. Who would not have them? To keep chaff out of a bushel, one sure plan is to fill it full of wheat. To keep out vain thoughts, it is wise and prudent to have the mind stored with choice subjects for meditation; these are easy to find, and we should never be without them. May we all be able to say with David, "In the multitude of my thoughts within me, thy comforts delight my soul."

Faults

HE WHO BOASTS of being perfect is perfect in folly. I have been a good deal up and down in the world, and I never did see either a perfect horse or a perfect man. I never shall till two Sundays come together. You cannot get white flour out of a coal sack, nor perfection out of human nature; he who looks for it had better look for sugar in the sea. The old saying is, "Lifeless, faultless." Of dead men we should say nothing but good, but as for the living, they are all tarred more or less with the black brush. Every head has a soft place in it, and every heart has its black drop. Every rose has its prickles, and every day its night. Even the sun shows spots, and the skies are darkened with clouds. Nobody is so wise but he has folly enough to stock a stall at Vanity Fair. Where I could not see the fool's-cap, I have nevertheless heard the bells jingle. As there is no sunshine without some shadows, so is all human good mixed up with more or less of evil. Even poor law guardians have their little failings, and servants of the Church are not wholly of heavenly nature. The best wine has it sediment. All men's faults are not written on their foreheads, and it's quite as well they are not, or hats would need very wide brims. As sure as eggs are eggs, faults of some sort nestle in every bosom. There is no telling when a man's sins may show themselves. Hares pop out of the ditch just when you are not looking for them. A horse that is weak in the legs may not stumble for a mile or two, but it is in him, and the rider had better hold him up well. The tabby cat is not lapping milk just now, but leave the dairy door open, and see if she is not as bad a thief as the kitten. There is fire in the flint, cool as it looks; wait till the steel gets a knock at it, and you will see. It is not everybody that will remember to keep his gunpowder out of the way of the candle.

If we would always remember that we live among men who are imperfect, we should not be in such a fever when we find out our friends' failings. Blessed is he who expects nothing of poor flesh and blood, for he shall never be disappointed. The best of men are men at the best, and the best wax will melt.

> It is a good horse that never stumbles,
> And a good wife that never grumbles.

But surely such horses and wives are only found in the fool's paradise, where dumplings grow on trees. In this wicked world the straightest timber has knots in it, and the cleanest field of wheat has its share of weeds. The most careful driver one day upsets the cart, the cleverest cook spills a little broth. I know to my sorrow a very decent plowman will now and then break the plow, and often make a crooked furrow. It is foolish to turn off a tried friend because of a failing or two. Being all of us full of faults, we ought to keep two bears, and learn to bear and forbear with one another. Since we all live in glass houses, we should none of us throw stones. Everybody laughs when the saucepan says to the kettle, "How black you are!" Other men's imperfections show us our imperfections, for one sheep is much like another. If there is an apple in my neighbor's eye, there is no doubt one in mine. We ought to use our neighbors as looking

FAULTS

glasses to see our own faults in, and mend in ourselves what we see in them.

I have no patience with those who poke their noses into every man's house to smell out his faults, and put on magnifying glasses to discover their neighbors' flaws. Such folks had better look at home, they might see the Devil where they little expected. What we wish to see we shall see, or think we see. Faults are always thick where love is thin. A white cow is all black if your eye chooses to make it so. If we sniff long enough at rose water, we shall find out that it has a bad smell. It would be a far more pleasant business, at least for other people, if fault hunters would turn their dogs to hunt out the good points in other folks. The game would pay better, and nobody would stand with a pitchfork to keep the huntsmen off his farm. As for our own faults, it would take a large slate to hold the account of them, but, thank God, we know where to take them. With all our faults, God loves us still if we are trusting in His Son. Therefore let us not be downhearted, but hope to live and learn, and do some good service before we die. Though the cart creaks it will get home with its load, and the old horse, broken-kneed as he is, will do a sight of work yet. There is no use in lying down and doing nothing because we cannot do everything as we should like. Faults or no faults, plowing must be done, and imperfect people must do it too, or there will be no harvest next year. Bad plowman as John may be, the angels will not do his work for him, and so he is off to do it himself.

Things Not Worth Trying

THAT IS A WISE OLD SAYING: "Spend not all you have; believe not all you hear; tell not all you know, and do not all you can." There is so much work to be done that needs our hands that it is a pity to waste a grain of our strength. When the game is not worth the candle, drop it at once. It is wasting time to look for milk in a gatepost, or blood in a turnip, or sense in a fool. Never ask a covetous man for money till you have boiled a flint soft. Do not sue a debtor who has not a penny; you will only be throwing good money after bad, which is like losing your ferret without getting a rabbit. Never offer a looking glass to a blind man: if a man is so proud that he will not see his faults, he will only quarrel with you for pointing them out to him. It is of no use to hold a lantern to a mole, or to talk of Heaven to a man who cares for nothing but his dirty money. There is a time for everything, and it is a silly thing to preach to drunken men, it is casting pearls before swine. Get them sober, and then talk to them soberly; if you lecture them while they are drunk, you act as if you were drunk.

Do not put a cat on a driver's seat, or men in places for which they are not fitted. There's no making apples of plums: little minds will still be little, even if you make them churchwardens. It is a pity to turn a monkey into a minister, or a maidservant into a mistress. Many preachers are good tailors spoiled, and capital shoemakers turned out of their proper calling. When God means a

THINGS NOT WORTH TRYING

creature to fly, He gives it wings. When He intends men to preach He gives them abilities. It is a pity to push a man into the war if he cannot fight. Better discourage a man's climbing than help him to break his neck. Silk purses are not to be made out of sows' ears. Pigs will never play well on the flute, teach them as long as you like.

It is not wise to aim at impossibilities—it is a waste of powder to fire at the man in the moon. Making unfinished boards out of sawdust is a very sensible scheme compared with what some of my friends have been aiming at, for they have been trying to get money by buying shares in companies. They might quite as soon catch the wind in a net, or carry water in a sieve. Bubbles are fine fun for boys, but bubble companies are edged tools that none should play with. If my friend has money which he can afford to lose, there is still no reason why he should hand it over to a set of rascals: if I wanted to get rid of my leg, I should not get a shark to snap it off. Give your money to fools sooner than let rogues wheedle you out of it.

It is never worth while to do unnecessary things. Never grease a fat sow or praise a proud man. Do not make clothes for fishes, or coverings for altars. Do not paint lilies or garnish the gospel. Never bind up a man's head before it is broken, or comfort a conscience that makes no confession. Never hold up a candle to show the sun, or try to prove a thing which nobody doubts. I would advise no one to attempt a thing which will cost more than it is worth. You may sweeten refuse with lavender water, and a bad living man may keep up a good character by an outward show of religion, but it will turn out a losing business in the long run. If the nation were sensible, it would sweep out a good many expensive but useless people, who eat the malt which lies in the house that Jack built; they live on the nation, but do it little service. To pay a man a pound for earning a penny is a good deal wiser than keeping bishops who meet together by the score and consult about the best way of doing nothing. If my master's old dog were as sleepy as some bishops are, he would get shot or drowned, for he would not be worth the amount of the dog tax. However, their time of reckoning is on the road, as sure as Christmas is coming.

Long ago my experience taught me not to dispute with anybody about tastes and whims. One might as well argue about what you can see in the fire. It is of no use plowing the air, or trying to convince a man against his will in matters of no consequence. It is useless to try to end a quarrel by getting angry over it; it is much the same as pouring oil on a fire to quench it, and blowing coals with the bellows to put them out. Some people like rows—I do not envy their choice; I'd rather walk ten miles to get out of a dispute than half-a-mile to get into one. I have often been told to be bold, and take the bull by the horns, but, as the amusement is more pleasant than profitable, I shall leave it to those who are so cracked already that an ugly poke with a horn would not damage their skulls. Solomon says: "Leave off strife before it be meddled with," which is much the same as if he had said, "Leave off before you begin." When you see a mad dog, do not argue with him unless you are sure of your logic. Better get out of his way, and if anybody calls you a coward, you need not call him a fool—everybody knows that. Meddling in quarrels never answers; let hornets' nests alone. Don't pull down old houses over your own head. Meddlers are sure to hurt their own characters; if you scrub other people's pigs, you will soon

THINGS NOT WORTH TRYING

need scrubbing yourself. It is the height of folly to interfere between a man and his wife, for they will be sure to leave off fighting each other and turn their whole strength upon you—and serve you right too. If you will put your spoon into other people's broth, and it scalds you, who is to blame but yourself?

One thing more, do not attempt to make a strongheaded woman give way, but remember—

> If she will, she will, you may depend on't:
> If she won't, she won't, and there's an end on't.

I cut out of a newspaper a scrap from America: "Dip the Mississippi dry with a teaspoon; twist your heel into the toe of your boot; send up fishinghooks with balloons and fish for stars; get astride a gossamer and chase a comet; when a rain storm is coming down like the cataract of Niagara, remember where you left your umbrella; choke a flea with a brickbat! In short, prove everything hitherto considered impossible to be possible—but never attempt to coax a woman to say she will when she has made up her mind to say she won't."

Debt

WHEN I WAS A VERY SMALL BOY, and went to a woman's school, it so happened that I wanted a slate pencil, and had no money to buy it. I was afraid of being scolded for losing my pencils so often, for I was real careless, and so did not dare to ask at home; what then was John to do? There was a little shop where nuts, and tops, and cakes, and balls were sold by old Mrs. Dearson. Sometimes I had seen boys and girls trusted by the old lady. I argued with myself that Christmas was coming, and that somebody or other would be sure to give me a penny then. I would, therefore, go into debt for a slate pencil, and be sure to pay at Christmas. I did not feel easy about it, but still I screwed my courage up and went into the shop. As I had never owed anything before, and my credit was good, the pencil was handed over by the kind dame, and *I was in debt*. It did not please me much, and I felt as if I had done wrong, but I little knew how soon I should smart for it. How my father heard of this little stroke of business I never knew, but some little bird or other whistled it to him, and he was very soon down upon me in earnest. God bless him for it; he was a sensible man, and none of your children spoilers. He did not intend to bring up his children to speculate, and play at what big men call financing, and therefore he knocked my getting into debt on the head at once. He gave me a very powerful lecture upon getting into debt, and how like it was to stealing; upon the way in which people were ruined by it; how a boy who would owe a little, might one day owe much, and get into prison, and bring his family into disgrace. It was a lecture, indeed. Then I was marched off to the shop like a deserter marched into barracks, crying bitterly as I went, and feeling dreadfully ashamed, because I thought everybody knew I was in debt. The money was paid amid many solemn warnings, and the poor debtor was set free, like a bird let out of a cage. How sweet it felt to be out of debt! How did my little heart vow and declare that nothing should ever tempt me into debt again! It was a fine lesson, and I have never forgotten it. If all boys were inoculated with the same doctrine when they were young, it would be as good as a fortune to them, and save them loads of trouble in after life. God bless my father, say I, and send such fathers to save us from being eaten up with villainy.

Ever since that early sickening I have hated debt, and if I say some fierce things about it, you must not wonder. To keep debt, dirt, and the Devil out of my cottage has been my greatest wish ever since I set up housekeeping. Although the last of the three has sometimes got in by the door or the window, for the old serpent will wriggle through the smallest crack, yet, thanks to a good wife, hard work, honesty, and scrubbing brushes, the two others have not crossed the threshold. Debt is so degrading, that if I owed a man a penny I would walk twenty miles, in winter, to pay him, sooner than feel that I was under an obligation. I should be as comfortable with peas in my shoes, or a hedgehog in my bed, or a snake up my back, as with bills hanging over my head at the grocer's, and the baker's, and the tailor's. Poverty is hard, but debt is horrible. A man might as well have a smoky house and a scolding wife, which are said to be the two worst evils of our life. We may be poor, and yet respectable, which John Ploughman and wife hope they are and will be; but a man in debt cannot even respect himself. He is sure to be talked about by the neighbors, and that talk will not be much to his credit. Some persons appear to like owing money; but I would as soon be a cat up a chimney with the fire going, or a fox with the hounds at my heels, or a hedgehog on a pitchfork, or a mouse under an owl's claw. An honest man thinks a purse full of other people's money to be worse than an empty one; he cannot bear to eat other people's cheese, wear other people's shirts, and walk about in other people's shoes. Neither will he be easy while his wife is decked out in the milliner's bonnets. The jackdaw in the peacock's feathers was soon plucked, and borrowers will surely come to poverty—a poverty of the bitterest sort, because there is shame in it.

Living beyond their incomes is the ruin of many of my neighbors; they can hardly afford to keep a rabbit, and must needs drive a pony. I am afraid extravagance is the common disease of the times, and many professing Christians have caught it, to their shame and sorrow. Girls must have silks and satins, and then there's a bill at the dressmaker's as long as a winter's night, and quite as dismal. Show, and style, and smartness run away with a man's means, keep the family poor, and the father's nose down on the grindstone. Frogs try to look as big as bulls, and burst themselves. Men burn the candle at both ends, and then say they are very unfortunate—why don't they put the saddle on the right horse, and say they are extravagant? Economy is half the battle in life; it is not so hard to earn money as to spend it well. Hundreds would never have known *want* if they had not first

DEBT

known *waste*. If all poor men's wives knew how to cook, how far a little might go! Our minister says the French and the Germans beat us in nice cheap cookery. I wish they would send missionaries over to convert gossiping women into good managers. This is a French fashion which would be a deal more useful than those fine pictures in Mrs. Frippery's window, with ladies rigged out in a new style every month. Dear me! some people are much too fine nowadays to eat what their fathers were thankful to see on the table. They please their palates with costly feeding, come to the poorhouse, and expect everybody to pity them. They turned up their noses at bread and butter, and came to eat raw turnips stolen out of the fields. They who live like fighting cocks at other men's costs will get their combs cut, or perhaps get roasted for it one of these days. If you have a great store of peas, you may put the more in the soup; but everybody should fare according to his earnings. He is both a fool and a rascal who has a quarter coming in, and on the strength of it spends five dollars which does not belong to him. "Cut your coat according to your cloth" is sound advice. Cutting other people's cloth by running into debt is like thieving. If I meant to be a rogue I would deal in marine stores, or be a pettifogging lawyer, or open a loan office, or go out picking pockets, but I would scorn the art of getting into debt without a prospect of being able to pay.

Debtors can hardly help being liars, for they promise to pay when they know they cannot. When they have made up a lot of false excuses they promise again, and so they lie as fast as a horse can trot.

> You have debts, and make debts still,
> If you've not lied, lie you will.

Now, if owing leads to lying, who shall say that it is

not a most evil thing? Of course, there are exceptions, and I do not want to bear hard upon an honest man who is brought down by sickness or heavy losses; but take the rule as a rule, and you will find debt to be a great dismal swamp, a huge mud-hole, a dirty ditch. Happy is the man who gets out of it after once tumbling in, but happiest of all is he who has been by God's goodness kept out of the mire. If you once ask the Devil to dinner it will be hard to get him out of the house again; better to have nothing to do with him. Where a hen has laid one egg she is very likely to lay another; when a man is once in debt, he is likely to get into it again; better keep clear of it from the first. He who gets in over shoes is very liable to be over boots.

If you want to sleep soundly, buy a bed of a man who is in debt; surely it must be a very soft one, or he never could have rested so easy on it. I suppose people get hardened to it, as Smith's donkey did when its master broke so many sticks across its back. It seems to me that a real honest man would sooner get as lean as a greyhound than feast on borrowed money. He would choke up his throat with March dust before he would let the landlord make chalks against him. What pins and needles tradesmen's bills must stick in a fellow's soul! A pig on credit always grunts. Without debt, without care; out of debt, out of danger; but owing and borrowing are bramble bushes full of thorns. If ever I borrow a spade of my next door neighbor I never feel safe with it for fear I should break it. I never can dig in peace as I do with my own; but if I had a spade at the shop and knew I could not pay for it, I think I should dig my own grave out of shame. Scripture says, "Owe no man anything," which does not mean pay your debts, but never have any to pay. My opinion is, that those who break this law ought to be turned out of the Christian church. Our laws are shamefully full of encouragement to credit: nobody need be a thief now; he has only to open a shop and make a failure of it, and it will pay him much better. The proverb is: "He who never fails will never grow rich." Why, I know tradesmen who have failed five or six times, and yet think they are on the road to Heaven. What would they do if they got there? They are a deal more likely to go where they shall never come out till they have paid the uttermost farthing. But people say, "How liberal they are!" Yes, with other people's money. I hate to see a man steal a goose and then give religion the giblets. Piety by all means, but pay your way as part of it. Honesty first, and then generosity. But how often religion is a cloak for deceiving! There's Mrs. Scamp as fine as a peacock, all the girls out at boarding-school, learning French and the piano, the boys swelling about in gloves, and G. B. Scamp, Esq., driving a fast-trotting mare, and taking the chair at public meetings, while his poor creditors cannot get more than enough to live from hand to mouth. It is shameful and beyond endurance to see how genteel swindling is winked at by many. If I had my way, I'd give them the county crop, and the prison garb for six months; gentlemen or not, I'd let them see that big rogues could dance on the treadmill to the same tune as little ones. I'd make the land too hot to hold such scamping gentry if I were a member of Parliament, or a prime minister. As I've no such power, I can at least let off the steam of my wrath in that way.

My motto is, pay as you go, and keep from small scores. Short reckonings are soon cleared. Pay what you owe, and what you're worth you'll know. Let the clock tick, but no *"tick"* for me. Better go to bed without your supper than get up in debt. Sins and debts are always more than we think them to be. Little by little a man gets over head and ears. It is the petty expenses that empty the purse. Money rolls away easily. Tom Thriftless buys what he does not want because it is a great bargain, and so is soon brought to sell what he does want, and find it a very little bargain. He cannot say "No" to his friend who wants him to be security; he gives grand dinners, makes many holidays, keeps a fat table, lets his wife dress fine, and by-and-by he is quite surprised to find that quarter-days come round so very fast, and that creditors bark so loud. He has sowed his money in the fields of thoughtlessness, and now he wonders that he has to reap the harvest of poverty. Still he hopes for something to turn up to help him out of difficulty, and so muddles himself into more troubles, forgetting that hope and expectation are a fool's income. Being hard up, he goes to market with empty pockets, and buys at whatever prices tradesmen like to charge him, and so he pays more than double and gets deeper and deeper into the mire. This leads him to scheming, and trying little tricks and mean dodges, for it is hard for an empty sack to stand upright. This is sure not to answer. Schemes are like spiders' webs, which never catch anything better than flies, and are soon swept away. As well attempt to mend your shoes with brown paper, or stop a broken window with a sheet of ice, as try to patch up a falling business with maneuvering and scheming. When the schemer is found out, he is like a dog in church, which everybody is after, and like a barrel of powder, which nobody wants for a neighbor.

They say poverty is a sixth sense, and it had need be, for many debtors seem to have lost the other five, or were born without common sense. They appear to fancy that you not only make debts, but pay them by borrowing. A man pays Peter with what he has borrowed of Paul, and thinks he is getting out of his difficulties. He is only putting one foot into the mud to pull his other foot out. It is hard to shave an egg, or pull hairs out of a bald pate, but they are both easier than paying debts out of an empty pocket. Samson was a strong man, but he could not pay debts without money. He is a fool who thinks he can do it by scheming. Jews and Gentiles, when they lend money, generally pluck the geese as long as they have any feathers. A man must cut down his outgoings and save his incomings if he wants to clear himself; you cannot spend your penny and pay debts with it too. Stint the kitchen if the purse is bare. Do not believe in any way of wiping out debts except by paying hard cash. Promises make debts, and debts make promises, but promises never pay debts. Promising is one thing, and performing is quite another. A good man's word should be as binding as an oath. He should never promise to pay unless he has a clear prospect of doing so in due time. Those who stave off payment by false promises, deserve no mercy. It is all very well to say "I'm very sorry," but—

> A hundred years of regret
> Pay not a farthing of debt.

Now I'm afraid all this sound advice might as well have been given to my master's cocks and hens as to those who have got into the way of spending what is not their own. Advice to such people goes in at one ear and out at the other; well, those who will not listen will have to feel, and those who refuse cheap advice will have to buy dear repentance. To young people beginning life, a word may be worth a world.

Home

THAT WORD *home* always sounds like poetry to me. It rings like a peal of bells at a wedding, only more soft and sweet, and it chimes deeper into the ears of my heart. It does not matter whether it means thatched cottage or manor house, home is home, be it ever so homely, and there's no place on earth like it. Green grow the houseleek on the roof forever, and let the moss flourish on the thatch. Sweetly the sparrows chirrup and the swallows twitter around the chosen spot which is my joy and rest. Every bird loves its own nest; the owl thinks the old ruins the fairest spot under the moon, and the fox is of opinion that his hole in the hill is remarkably cozy. When my master's horse knows that his head is toward home he wants no whip, but thinks it best to put on all steam. I am always of the same mind, for the way home to me is the best bit of road in the country. I like to see the smoke out of my own chimney better than the fire on another man's hearth; there's something so beautiful in the way in which it curls up among the trees. Cold potatoes on my own table taste better than roast meat at my neighbor's, and the honeysuckle at my own door is the sweetest I ever smell. When you go out, friends do their best, but still it is not home. "Make yourself at home," they say, because everybody knows that to feel at home is to feel at ease.

> East and west,
> Home is best.

HOME

Why, at home you are at home, and what more do you want? Nobody grudges you, whatever your appetite may be; and you do not get put into a damp bed. Safe in his own castle, like a king in his palace, a man feels himself somebody, and is not afraid of being thought proud for thinking so. Every cock may crow on his own dunghill; and a dog is a lion when he is at home. A chimney sweep is master inside his own door. No need to guard every word because some enemy is on the watch, no keeping the heart under lock and key. As soon as the door is shut it is liberty hall, and none to peep and pry. I could show you something which to my mind is real beauty: I mean John Ploughman's cottage, with the kettle boiling on the hob, singing like an unfallen black angel, while the cat is lying asleep in front of the fire, and the wife in her chair mending stockings, and the children about the room, as full of fun as young lambs. It is a singular fact, and perhaps some of you will doubt it, but that is your unbelieving nature, our little ones are real beauties, always a pound or two plumper than others of their age, and yet it doesn't tire you half so much to nurse them as it does other people's babies. Why, bless you, my wife would play out in half the time, if her neighbor had asked her to see to a strange youngster, but her own children don't seem to tire her at all. My belief is that it all comes of their having been born at home. Just so is it with everything else: our lane is the most beautiful for twenty miles round, because our home is in it; and my garden is a perfect paradise, for no other particular reason than this very good one, that it belongs to the old house at home.

I cannot make out why so many working men spend their evenings at a public house, when their own fireside would be so much better and cheaper too. There they sit, hour after hour, talking nonsense, and forgetting the dear good souls at home who are half starved and weary with waiting for them. Their money goes into the publican's till when it ought to make their wives and children comfortable. The liquor they get is just so much fools' milk to drown their wits in. Liquor shops are a curse of this country—no good ever can come of them, and the evil they do no tongue can tell. I wish the man who made the law to open them had to keep all the families that they have brought to ruin. Poor men do not need such places, nor rich men either, they are all worse and no better. Anything that hurts the home is a curse, and ought to be hunted down.

Husbands should try to make home happy and holy. It is an ill bird that fouls its own nest, a bad man who makes his home wretched. Our house ought to be a little church, with holiness to the Lord over the door, but it ought never to be a prison where there is plenty of rule and order, but little love and no pleasure. Married life is not all sugar, but grace in the heart will keep away most of the sours. Godliness and love can make a man, like a bird in a hedge, sing among thorns and briers, and set others singing too. It should be the husband's pleasure to please his wife, and the wife's care to care for her husband. He is kind to himself who is kind to his wife. I am afraid some men live by the rule of self, and when that is the case home happiness is a mere sham. When husbands and wives are well yoked, how light their load becomes! It is not every couple that is a pair, and the more's the pity. In a true home all the strife is which can do the most to make the family happy. A home should be a Bethel, not a Babel. The husband should be the houseband, binding all together like a corner stone, but not crushing everything like a mill-stone. Un-

HOME

kind and domineering husbands ought not to pretend to be Christians, for they act clean contrary to Christ's commands. Yet a home must be well ordered, or it will become a Bedlam. If the father drops the reins, the family-coach will soon be in the ditch. A wise mixture of love and firmness will do it: but neither harshness nor softness alone will keep home in happy order. Home is no home where the children are not in obedience, it is rather a pain than a pleasure to be in it. Happy is he who is happy in his children, and happy are the children who are happy in their father. All fathers are not wise. Some are like Eli, and spoil their children. Not to cross our children is the way to make a cross of them. Those who never give their children the rod must not wonder if their children become a rod to them. Solomon says, "Correct thy son, and he shall give thee rest; yea, he shall give delight to thy soul." I am not clear that anybody wiser than Solomon lives in our time, though some think they are. Young colts must be broken in or they will make wild horses. Some fathers are all fire and fury, filled with passion at the smallest fault; this is worse than the other, and makes home a little hell instead of a heaven. No wind makes the miller idle, but too much upsets the mill altogether. Men who strike in their anger generally miss their mark. When God helps us to hold the reins firmly, but not to hurt the horses' mouths, all goes well. When home is ruled according to God's Word, angels might be asked to stay a night with us, and they would not find themselves out of their element.

Wives should feel that home is their place and their kingdom, the happiness of which depends mostly upon them. She is a wicked wife who drives her husband away by her tongue. A man said to his wife the other day, "Double up your whip;" he meant, keep your tongue quiet: it is wretched living with such a whip always lashing you. When God gave to men ten measures of speech, they say the women ran away with nine, and in some cases I am afraid the saying is true. A dirty, slatternly, gossiping wife is enough to drive her husband mad. If he goes out of an evening, she is the cause of it. It is doleful living where the wife, instead of reverencing her husband, is always wrangling and railing at him. It must be a good thing when such women are hoarse, and it is a pity that they have not as many blisters on their tongues as they have teeth in their jaws. God save us from wives who are angels in the streets, saints in the church, and devils at home. I have never tasted of such bitter herbs, but I pity from my very heart those who have this diet every day.

Show me a loving husband, a worthy wife, and good children, and nothing could take me in a year where I could see a more pleasing sight. Home is the grandest of all institutions. Give me a quiet little parlor. Boast about voting and reform bills if you like, but I go in for weeding the little garden, and teaching the children their hymns. Franchise may be a very fine thing, but I should a good deal sooner get the freehold of my cottage, if I could find the money to buy it. Magna Charta I don't know much about, but if it means a quiet home for everybody, three cheers for it.

If I had no home the world would be a big prison to me. These times make a man think of his wings, but I am tied by the leg to my own home, and, please God, I hope to live and die among my people.

Men Who Are Down

No man's lot is fully known till he is dead: change of fortune is the lot of life. He who rides in a carriage may yet have to clean it. He who is up aloft may have to take his turn in the pit. In less than a thousand years we shall all be bald and poor too, and who knows what he may come to before that? The thought that we may ourselves be one day under the window should make us careful when we are throwing out dirty water. With what measure we mete it shall be measured to us again, therefore let us look well to our dealings with the unfortunate.

Nothing makes me more sick of human nature than to see the way in which men treat others when they fall down the ladder of fortune. "Down with him," they cry, "he always was good for nothing."

> Down among the dead men, down, down, down,
> Down among the dead men, there let him lie.

Dog won't eat dog, but men will eat each other like cannibals, and boast of it too. There are thousands in this world who fly like vultures to feed on a tradesman or a merchant as soon as ever he gets into trouble. Where the carcass is, thither will the eagles be gathered together. Instead of a little help, they give the sinking man a great deal of cruelty, and cry, "Serves him right." All the world will beat the man whom fortune buffets. If providence smites him, all men's whips begin to crack. The dog is drowning, and therefore all his friends empty their buckets over him. The tree has fallen, and everybody runs for his hatchet. The house is on fire, and all the neighbors warm themselves. The man has ill luck, therefore his friends give him ill usage; he has tumbled into the road, and they drive their carts over him: he is down, and selfishness cries, "Let him be kept down, then there will be the more room for those who are up."

How aggravating it is when those who knocked you down kick you for not standing up! It is not very pleasant to hear that you have been a fool. There were fifty ways at least of keeping out of your difficulty, only you had not the sense to see them. You ought not to have lost the game; even Tom Fool can see where you made a bad move. *"He ought to have locked the stable door"*; everybody can see that, but nobody offers to buy the loser a new horse. *"What a pity he went so far on the ice!"* That's very true, but that won't save the poor fellow from drowning. When a man's coat is threadbare, it is an easy thing to pick a hole in it. Good advice is poor food for a hungry family.

> A man of words and not of deeds,
> Is like a garden full of weeds.

Lend me a bit of string to tie up the traces, and find fault with my old harness when I get home. Help my old horse to a few oats, and then tell him to mend his pace. Feel for me, and I shall be much obliged to you. Mind you feel in your pocket, or else a fig for your feelings.

Most men who go down hill meet with Judas before they get to the bottom. Those whom they helped in their better days generally forget the debt, or repay it with unkindness. The young sucker runs away with the sap from the old tree. The foal drains his mother, and then kicks her. The old saying is: "I taught you to swim, and now you would drown me," and many a time it comes true. The dog wags his tail till he gets the bone, and then he snaps and bites at the man who fed him. Eaten bread is forgotten, and the hand that gave it is despised. The candle lights others and is burnt away itself. For the most part, nothing is more easily blotted out than a good turn. Everyone for himself is the world's golden rule, and we all know who takes the hindmost. The fox looks after his own skin, and has no idea of losing his brush out of gratitude to a friend.

A noble spirit always takes the side of the weak, but noble spirits do not often ride along our roads; they are as scarce as eagles. You can get magpies, and hawks, and kites by the score, but the nobler breed you don't see once in a lifetime. Did you ever hear the crows read the burial service over a dead sheep before they eat it? Well, that's wonderfully like the neighbors crying, "What a pity! How did it happen? Oh, dear! Oh dear!" and then falling to work to get each of them a share of the plunder. Most people will help those who do not need it; every traveler throws a stone where there is a heap already; the cooks baste the fat pig, and the lean one gets burned.

> In times of prosperity friends will be plenty:
> In times of adversity not one in twenty.

When the wind serves, all aid. While the pot boils, friendship blooms. But flatterers haunt not cottages, and the faded rose no suitor knows. All the neighbors are cousins to the rich man, but the poor man's brother does not know him. When we have a ewe and a lamb, every one cries, "Welcome, Peter!" The squire can be heard for half-a-mile, if he only whispers, but Widow Needy is not heard across the park railings, let her call as she may.

Men willingly pour water into a full tub, and give feasts to those who are not hungry, because they look to have as good or better in return. Have a goose and get a goose. Have a horse of your own, and then you can borrow one. It is safe to lend barley where the barn is full of wheat, but who lends or gives where there's none? Who, indeed, unless it be some antiquated old soul who believes in his Bible, and loves his Lord, and therefore gives, "hoping for nothing again"?

I have noticed certain people who pretend to be great friends to a falling man because there are some few pickings yet to be got off his bones. The lawyer and the moneylender will cover the poor fellow with their wings, and then peck at him with their bills till there's nothing left. When these folks are very polite and considerate, poor men had need beware. It was not a good sign when the fox walked into the hen-house and said, "Good morning to you all, my very dear friends."

Men who are down, however, must not despair, for God is yet alive, and he is the friend of the friendless. If there be no one else found to hold out a hand to him who has fallen, the Lord's hand shall not fail to bring deliverance to those who trust Him. A good man may be put in the fire, but he cannot be burned. His hope may be drenched but not drowned. He plucks up courage and sets a stout heart to a stiff hill, and gets over rough ground where others lie down and die. While there's life there's hope. Therefore, my friend, if you have tumbled off the back of prosperity, John Ploughman bids you not to lie in the ditch, but up and try again. Jonah went to the bottom of the sea, but he got to shore again all the better for his watery journey.

MEN WHO ARE DOWN

> Though the bird's in the net,
> It may get away yet;
> Though I'm down in the dust,
> In my God I will trust,
> I will hope in Him still,
> And leave all to His will;
> For He'll surely appear,
> And will banish my fear.

Let it never be forgotten that when a man is down he has a grand opportunity for trusting God. A false faith can only float in smooth water, but true faith, like a lifeboat, is at home in storms. If our religion does not bear us up in time of trial what is the use of it? If we cannot believe God when our circumstances appear to be against us we do not believe Him at all. We trust a thief as far as we can see him, shall we dare to treat our God in that fashion? No, no. The Lord is good, and He will yet appear for His servants, and we shall praise His name.

> Down among the dead men! No, sir, not I.
> Down among the dead men! I will not lie.
> Up among the hopeful I will ascend,
> Up among the joyful sing without end.

Hope

EGGS ARE EGGS, but some are rotten; hopes are hopes, but many of them are delusions. Hopes are like women, there is a touch of angel about them all, but there are two sorts. My boy Tom has been blowing a lot of birds'-eggs, and threading them on a string; I have been doing the same thing with hopes. Here's a few of them, good, bad and indifferent.

The sanguine man's hope pops up in a moment like jack-in-the-box. It works with a spring, and does not go by reason. Whenever this man looks out of the window he sees better times coming. Although it is nearly all in his own eye, and nowhere else, yet to see plum puddings in the moon is a far more cheerful habit than croaking at everything like a two-legged frog. This is the kind of brother to be on the road with on a dark night, when it pours with rain, for he carries candles in his eyes and a fireside in his heart. Beware of being misled by him, and then you may safely keep his company. His fault is that he counts his chickens before they are hatched, and sells his herrings before they are in the net. All his sparrow's-eggs are bound to turn into thrushes, at the least, if not partridges and pheasants. Summer has fully come, for he has seen one swallow. He is sure to make his fortune at his new shop, for he had not opened the door five minutes before two of the neighbors crowded in, one of them wanted a loaf of bread on trust, and the other asked change for some money. He is certain that

HOPE

the squire means to give him his trade, for he saw him reading the name over the shop door as he rode past. He does not believe in slips between cups and lips, but makes certainties out of perhapses. Well, good soul, though he is a little soft at times, there is much in him to praise. I like to think of one of his odd sayings, "Never say *die* till you are dead, and then it's no use, so let it alone." There are other odd people in the world, you see, besides John Ploughman.

My neighbor Shiftless is waiting for his aunt to die, but the old lady has as many lives as nine cats, and my notion is that when she does die she will leave her little money to the Hospital for Diseased Cats or Stray Dogs, sooner than her nephew shall have it. He is dreadfully down at the heel, and lays it all on the dear old lady's provoking constitution. However, he hopes on, and gets worse and worse, for while the grass grows the horse starves. He pulls at a long rope who waits for another's death; he who hunts after legacies had need have iron shoes. He that waits for dead men's shoes may long go barefoot; he who waits for his uncle's cow need not be in a hurry to spread the butter. He who lives on hope has a slim diet. If Jack Shiftless had never had an aunt he might have tucked up his shirt sleeves and worked for himself, but they told him that he was born with a silver spoon in his mouth. That made a spoon of him, so that he is no more use at work than a cow at catching hares. If anybody likes to leave John Ploughman a legacy, he will be very much obliged to him, but he had better not tell him of it for fear he should not plow so straight a furrow; they had better make it twice as much, and take him by surprise. On the whole, it would be better to leave it to the Pastors' College or an orphanage, for it will be well used in either case. I wish people would think less about windfalls, and plant more apple trees. Hopes that grow out of graves are grave mistakes; and when they cripple a man's own energies, they are a sort of hangman's rope, dangling round a man's neck.

Some people were born on the first of April, and are always hoping without sense or reason. Their ship is to come home; they are to dig up a pot of gold, or to hear of something to their advantage. Poor folk, they have wind on the brain, and dream while they are awake. They may hold their mouths open a long while before fried ham and eggs will come flying into them, yet they really seem to believe that some stroke of luck, some windfall of golden apples, will one day set them up and make something of them. They hope to ride in coaches, and by-and-by find themselves shut up in a place where the coaches won't run over them. You may whistle a long while before goldfinches will hop on to your thumb. Once in a while one man in a million may stumble against a fortune, but thousands ruin themselves by idle expectations. Expect to get half of what you earn, a quarter of what is your due, and none of what you have lent, and you will be near the mark. To look for a fortune to fall from the moon is to play the fool with a vengeance. A man ought to hope within the bounds of reason and the promises of the good old Book. Hope leans on an anchor, but an anchor must have something to hold by and to hold to. A hope without grounds is a tub without a bottom, a horse without a head, a goose without a body, a shoe without a sole, a knife without a blade. Who but Simple Simon would begin to build a house at the top? there must be a foundation. Hope is no hope, but sheer folly, when a man hopes for impossibilities, or looks for crops without sowing seed, and for happiness without doing good. Such hopes lead to great

HOPE

boast and small roast. They act like a jack-o'-lantern, and lead men into the ditch. There's poor Will at the poorhouse, who always declares that he owns a great estate, only the right owner keeps him out of it; his name is Jenyns, or Jennings, and somebody of that name he says has left enough money to buy the bank and one day he is to have a share of it. Meanwhile poor Will finds the broth poor stuff for such a great gentleman's stomach. He has promised me an odd thousand or two when he gets his fortune, and I am going to build a castle in the air with it, and ride to it on a broomstick. Poor soul, like a good many others, he has windmills in his head, and may make his will on his thumbnail for all that he has to give. Depend upon it, plowing the air is not half so profitable as it is easy: he who hopes in this world for more than he can get by his own earnings hopes to find apricots on a crab-tree. He who marries a slovenly, dressy girl, and hopes to make her a good wife, might well buy a goose and expect it to turn out a milch cow. Men cannot be in their senses when they set a wicked example and reckon upon raising a respectable family. You may hope and hope till your heart grows sick; but when you send your boy up the chimney, he will come down black for all your hoping. Teach a child to lie, and then hope that he will grow up honest; better put a wasp in a tar barrel and wait till he makes you honey. When will people act sensibly with boys and girls? Not till they are sensible themselves.

As to the next world, it is a great pity that men do not take a little more care when they talk of it. If a man dies drunk, somebody is sure to say, "I hope he is gone to Heaven." It is all very well to wish it, but to *hope* it is another thing. Men turn their faces to Hell and hope to get to Heaven; why don't they walk into the horsepond, and hope to be dry? Hopes of Heaven are solemn things, and should be tried by the Word of God. A man might as well hope, as our Lord says, to gather grapes of thorns or figs of thistles as look for a happy hereafter at the end of a bad life. There is only one Rock to build good hopes on, and that is not Peter, neither is it sacraments, but the merits of the Lord Jesus. All the hope of man is in "the man Christ Jesus." If we believe in Him we are saved, for it is written "he that believeth in him hath everlasting life." Mind he has it now, and it is *everlasting*, so that there is no fear of his losing it. There John Ploughman rests, and he is not afraid of being confounded, for this is a firm footing, and gives him a hope sure and steadfast, which neither life nor death can shake; but John must not turn preacher, or he may take the bread out of the parson's mouth, so please remember that presumption is a ladder which will break the mounter's neck, and don't try it, as you love your soul.

Spending

TO EARN MONEY is easy compared with spending it well; anybody may dig up potatoes, but it not one in ten that can cook them. Men do not become rich by what they get, but by what they save. Many men who have money are as short of wit as a hog is of wool. They are under the years of discretion though they have turned forty, and make ducks and drakes of hundreds as boys do of stones. What their fathers got with the rake they throw away with the shovel. After the miser comes the prodigal. Often men say of the spendthrift, his old father was no man's friend but his own, and now the son is no man's enemy but his own. The fact is, the old gentleman went to death by the lean road, and his son has made up his mind to go there by the fat. As soon as the spendthrift gets his estate it goes like a lump of butter in a greyhound's mouth. All his days are the first of April; he would buy an elephant at a bargain, or thatch his house with pancakes. Nothing is too foolish to tickle his fancy; his money burns holes in his pocket, and he must squander it, always boasting that his motto is, "Spend, and God will send." He will not stay till he has his sheep before he shears them; he forestalls his income, draws upon his capital, and so kills the goose which lays the golden eggs, and cries out, "Who would have thought it?" He never spares at the brim, but he means, he says, to save at the bottom. He borrows at high interest of Rob'em, Cheat'em, and Sell'em-up, and when he gets cleaned out, he lays it all either upon the lawyers or else on the bad times. Times never were good for lazy prodigals. If they were good to them they would be bad for all the world besides. Why men should be in such a hurry to make themselves beggars is a mystery, but nowadays, what with betting at horse races, laziness, and speculating, there seems to be a regular coach running to Needham every day. Ready money must be quite a curiosity to some men, and yet they spend like lords. They are gentlemen without means, which is much the same as plum-puddings without plums.

> Spending your money with many a guest,
> Empties the larder, the cellar, and chest.

If a little gambling is thrown in with fast living, money melts like a snowball in an oven. A young gambler is sure to be an old beggar if he lives long enough.

> The Devil leads him by the nose,
> Who the dice so often throws.

There are more asses than those with four legs. I am sorry to say they are found among working men as well as fine gentlemen. Fellows who have no estate but their labors, and no family arms except those they work with, will yet spend their little hard earnings in waste. No sooner are their wages paid than away they go to the "Spotted Dog," or the "Marquis of Granby," to contribute their share of fools' money toward keeping up the landlord. Drinking water neither makes a man sick nor in debt, nor his wife a widow; yet some men hardly know the flavor of it. Liquor guzzled down as it is by many a working man is nothing better than brown ruin. Men sit on the ale bench and wash out what little sense they ever had. I believe that farming people are a deal better managers with their money than city people are, for though their money be very little, their families look nice and tidy on Sundays. True, the rent isn't so bad in a village as in the city, and there's a bit of garden; still those city people earn money and have many chances of buying in a cheap market which the countryman has not. On the whole, I think 'tis very good management which keeps a family going on little in the country, and bad management that can't pay its way on much more in the city. Why, some families are as merry as mice in malt on very small wages; others are as wretched as rats in a trap on double the amount. Those who wear the shoe know best where it pinches, but economy is a fine thing. Some make soup out of a flint, and others cannot get nourishment out of gravy beef. Some go to shop with as much wit as Samson had in both his shoulders, but no more. They do not buy well; they have not sense to lay out their money to advantage. Buyers ought to have a hundred eyes, but these have not even one, and they do not open that; well was it said that if fools did not go to market bad wares would never be sold. They never get a pennyworth for their penny, and this often because they are on the hunt for cheap things. They forget that generally the cheapest is the dearest, and one cannot buy a good quarter's worth of a bad article. Poor men often buy in very small quantities, and so pay through the nose. A man who buys by the pennyworth keeps his own house and another man's. Why not get two or three weeks' supply at once, and get it cheaper? Store is no sore. People are often saving at the wrong place. Others look after small savings and forget greater things; they are penny wise and pound foolish; they spare at the spigot, and let all run away at the bunghole. Some buy things they do not want, because they are great bargains; let me tell them that what they do not want is dear at any price. Fine dressing makes a great hole in poor people's means. Whatever does John Ploughman, and such as work hard for their daily bread, want with silks and satins? It's like a blacksmith wearing a white silk apron. I hate to see a servant girl or a laborer's daughter tricked out as if she thought people would take her for a lady. Why everybody knows a tadpole from a fish; nobody mistakes a poppy for a rose. Give me a woman in a nice neat dress, clean and suitable, and for beauty she will beat the flashy young woman all to pieces. Buy what suits yourself to wear, and if it does not suit other people to look at, let them shut their eyes. All women are good—either for something or for nothing. Their dress will generally tell you which.

I suppose we all find the money goes quite fast enough, but after all it was made to circulate, and there's no use in hoarding it. It is bad to see our money become a runaway servant, and leave us. It would be worse to have it stop with us and become our master. We should try, as our minister says, "to find the golden mean," and neither be lavish nor stingy. He has his money best spent who has the best wife. The husband may earn money, but usually only the wife can save it. "A wise woman buildeth her house, but the foolish plucketh it down with her hands." The wife it seems, according to Solomon, is the builder or the real puller down. A man cannot prosper till he gets his wife's leave. A thrifty housewife is better than a great income. A good wife and health are a man's best wealth. Bless their hearts, what should we do without them? It is said they like to have their own way, but then the proverb says, a wife ought to have her will during life; she cannot make one when she dies.

A Good Word for Wives

WE PULLED UP THE HORSES in the last chapter at the sign of the "Good Woman." It is astonishing how many old sayings there are against wives, you may find nineteen to the dozen of them. Men years ago showed the rough side of their tongues whenever they spoke of their wives.

I recollect an old ballad that Gaffer Brooks used to sing about a man's being better hung than married; it shows how common it was to abuse married life.

Now this does not prove that the women are bad, but that their husbands are good for nothing, or else they would not make up slanders about their partners. There have, no doubt, been some shockingly bad wives in the world. But how many thousands have there been of true helpmeets, worth far more than their weight in gold! There is only one Job's wife mentioned in the Bible and one Jezebel, but there are no end of Sarahs and Rebekahs. I am of Solomon's mind, that, as a rule, he that findeth a wife findeth a good thing. If there's bad money taken at the grocer's, all the neighbors hear of it, but of the good report says nothing. A good woman makes no noise, and no noise is made about her, but a shrew is noted all over the parish. Taking them for all in all, they are most angelical creatures, and a great deal too good for half the husbands.

It is much to the women's credit that there are very few old sayings against husbands, although, in this case, sauce for the goose would make capital sauce for the gander. The mare has as good reasons for kicking as the horse has. They must be very forbearing. They may be rather quick in their talk, but is it not the nature of bells and belles to have tongues that swing easy? They cannot be so very bad after all, or they would have had their revenge for the many cruel things which are said against them. If they are a bit masterful, their husbands cannot be such very great victims, or they would surely have sense enough to hold their tongues about it. Men do not care to have it known when they are thoroughly henpecked, and I feel pretty certain that the old sayings are nothing but chaff. If they were true, men would never dare to own it.

A true wife is her husband's better half, his lump of delight, his flower of beauty, his guardian angel, and his heart's treasure. He says to her: "I shall in thee most happy be. In thee, my choice, I do rejoice. In thee I find content of mind. God's appointment is my contentment." In her company he finds his earthly heaven; she is the light of his home; the comfort of his soul, and (for this world) the soul of his comfort. Whatever fortune God may send him, he is rich so long as she lives.

A good husband makes a good wife. Some men can neither do without wives nor with them; they are wretched alone in what is called single blessedness, and they make their homes miserable when they get married. They are like Tompkin's dog, which could not bear to be loose, and howled when it was tied up. Happy bachelors are likely to be happy husbands, and a happy husband is the happiest of men. A well-matched couple carry a joyful life between them, as the two spies carried the cluster of Eschol. They multiply their joys by sharing them, and lessen their troubles by dividing them: this is fine arithmetic. The wagon of care rolls lightly along as they pull together. When it drags a little heavily, or there's a hitch anywhere, they love each other all the more, and so lighten the labor.

When a couple fall out there are always faults on both sides, and generally there is a pound on one and sixteen ounces on the other. When a home is miserable it is as often the husband's fault as the wife's. Darby is as much to blame as Joan, and sometimes more. If the husband will not keep sugar in the cupboard, no wonder his wife gets sour. Want of bread makes want of love; lean dogs fight. Poverty generally rides home on the husband's back, for it is not often the woman's place to go out working for wages. A man down our parts gave his wife a ring with this on it, "If thee don't work, thee shan't eat." It is no business of hers to bring in the grist —she is to see it is well used and not wasted. I say, short commons are not her fault. She is not the breadwinner, but the bread maker. She earns more at home than any wages she can get abroad.

It is not the wife who smokes and drinks away the wages at the "Brown Bear," or the "Jolly Topers." One sees a drunken woman now and then, and it's an awful sight, but in ninety-nine cases out of a hundred it is the man who comes home tipsy ,and abuses the children— the woman seldom does. The poor wife is a teetotaler, whether she likes it or not, and gets plenty of hot water as well as cold. Women are found fault with for often looking into the glass, but that is not so bad a glass as men drown their senses in. The wives do not sit over the tap-room fire; they are shivering at home with the baby, watching the clock (if there is one), wondering when their lords and masters will come home, and crying while they wait. I wonder they do not strike. Some of them are about as wretched as a mouse in a cat's mouth. They have to nurse the sick girl, and wash the dirty boy, and bear with the crying and noise of the children, while his lordship puts on his hat, and goes off about his own pleasure, or comes in at his own time to find fault with his wife for not getting him a fine supper. How could he expect to be fed like a fighting-cock when he brought home so little money on Saturday night, and spent so much in worshiping John Barleycorn? I say it, and I know it, there's many a house where there would be no scolding wife if there was not a skulking, guzzling husband. Fellows who are not fit drink and drink till all is blue, and then turn on their poor wives for not having more to give them. Do not tell me, I say it, and will maintain it, a woman cannot help being vexed when, with all her mending and striving, she cannot keep house because her husband will not let her. It would provoke any of us if we had to make bricks without straw, keep the pot boiling without fire, and pay the piper out of an empty purse. What can she get out of the oven when she has neither meal nor dough? Bad husbands are thoroughbred sneaks, and ought to be hung up by their heels till they know better.

They say a man of straw is worth a woman of gold, but I cannot swallow it. A man of straw is worth no more than a woman of straw; let old sayings lie as they like. Jack is no better than Jill, as a rule. When there is wisdom in the husband there's generally gentleness in the wife, and between them the old wedding wish is worked out: "One year of joy, another of comfort, and all the rest of content." Where hearts agree, there joy will be. United hearts death only parts. They say *marriage* is not often *merry-age,* but very commonly *mar-age.* If so, the coat and waistcoat have as much to do with it as the

A GOOD WORD FOR WIVES

gown and petticoat. The honeymoon need not come to an end. When it does it is often the man's fault for eating all the honey, and leaving nothing but moonshine. When they both agree whatever becomes of the moon they will each keep up their share of honey. When a man dwells under the sign of the cat's foot, where faces get scratched, either his wife did not marry a man or he did not marry a woman. If a man cannot take care of himself, his wit must be as scant as the wool of a blue dog. I do not pity most of the men martyrs; I save my pity for the women. Every herring must hang by its own gill, and every person must account for his own share in home quarrels, but John Ploughman cannot bear to see all the blame laid on the women. Whenever a dish is broken, the cat did it, and whenever there is mischief, there's a woman at the bottom of it. Here are two as pretty lies as you will meet within a month's march. There's a why for every wherefore, but the why for family jars does not always lie with the housekeeper. I know some women have long tongues, then the more's the pity that the husbands should set them going. For the matter of talk, just look into a tavern when the men's jaws are well oiled with liquor, and if any women living can talk faster or be more stupid my name is not John Ploughman.

When I got this far, in stepped our minister, and he said, "John, you've got a tough subject, a cut above you; I'll lend you a rare old book to help you over the stile."

"Well, sir," said I, "a little help is worth a great deal of fault-finding, and I shall be uncommonly obliged to you."

He sent me down old William Secker's "Wedding Ring," and a real wise fellow that Secker was. I could not do any other than pick out some of his pithy bits.

They are very flavory, and such as are likely to glue themselves to the memory. He says, "Hast thou a soft heart? It is of God's breaking. Hast thou a sweet wife? She is of God's making. The Hebrews have a saying, 'He is not a man that hath not a woman.' Though man alone may be good, yet it is not good that man should be alone. 'Every good gift and every perfect gift is from above.' A wife, though she be not a perfect gift, is a good gift. How happy are those marriages where Christ is at the wedding! Let none but those who have found favor in God's eyes find favor in yours. Husbands should spread a mantle of charity over their wives' infirmities. Husbands and wives should provoke one another to love, and they should love one another notwithstanding provocations. The tree of love should grow up in the midst of the family as the tree of life grew in the garden of Eden. Good servants are a great blessing; good children a greater blessing; but a good wife is the greatest blessing. Such a help let him seek for her that wants one; let him sigh for her that hath lost one; let him delight in her that enjoys one."

To come down from the old Puritan's roast beef to my own pot-herbs, or, as they say, to put Jack after gentleman, I will tell my own experience.

My experience of my first wife, who will I hope live to be my last, is much as follows: matrimony came from Paradise and leads to it. I never was half so happy before I was a married man as I am now. When you are married your bliss begins. I have no doubt that where there is much love there will be much to love, and where love is scant faults will be plentiful. If there is only one good wife in the country, I am the man who put the ring on her finger, and long may she wear it. God bless

A GOOD WORD FOR WIVES

the dear soul if she can put up *with* me, she shall never be put down *by* me.

If I were not married today, and saw a suitable partner, I would be married tomorrow morning before breakfast. What think you of that? "Why," says one, "I think John would get a new wife if he were left a widower." Well, and what if he did, how could he better show that he was happy with his first? I declare I would not say, as some do, that they married to have some one to look after the children. I should marry to have one to look after. John Ploughman is a sociable soul, and could not do in a house by himself.

Marriages are made in Heaven: matrimony in itself is good, but there are fools who turn meat into poison, and make a blessing into a curse. A man who has sought his wife from God, and married her for her character, and not merely for her figure head, may look for a blessing on his choice. They who join their love in God above, who pray to love, and love to pray, will find that love and joy will never cloy.

He who respects his wife will find that she respects him. With what measure he metes it shall be measured to him again, good measure, pressed down, and running over. He who consults his wife will have a good counselor. I have heard our minister say: "Women's instincts are often truer than man's reason;" they jump at a thing at once, and are wise offhand. Say what you will of your wife's advice, it's as likely as not you will be sorry you did not take it. So no more at present, as the thatcher said when he had *cleared* every dish on the table.

Men with Two Faces

EVEN BAD MEN praise consistency. Thieves like honest men. They are the best to rob. When you know where to find a man, he has one good point at any rate. A fellow who howls with the wolves, and bleats with the sheep, gets nobody's good word unless it be the Devil's. To carry two faces under one hat is, however, very common. Many look as if butter would not melt in their mouths, and yet can spit fire when it suits their purpose. I read an advertisement about reversible coats: the tailor who sells them must be making a fortune. Holding with the hare and running with the hounds is still in fashion. Consistency is about as scarce in the world as musk in a dog-kennel.

You may trust some men as far as you can see them, but no farther, for new company makes them new men. Like water, they boil or freeze according to the temperature. Some do this because they have no principles; they are of the weathercock persuasion, and turn with the wind. You might as well measure the moon for a suit of clothes as know what they are. They believe in that which pays best. They always put up at the Golden Fleece. Their mill grinds any grist which you bring to it if the ready money is forthcoming. They go with every wind, north, south, east, west, north-east, north-west, south-east, south-west, nor'-nor'-east, south-west-by-south, or any other in all the world. Like frogs, they can live on land or water, and are not at all particular which it is.

Like a cat, they always fall on their feet, and will stop anywhere if you butter their toes. They love their friends dearly, but their love lies in the cupboard, and if that be bare, like a mouse, their love runs off to some other larder. They say, "Leave you, dear girl? Never, while you have money." How they scuttle off if you come to failure! Like rats, they leave a sinking ship.

> When good cheer is lacking,
> Such friends will be packing.

Their heart follows the pudding. While the pot boils they sit by the fire; when the meal tray is empty they play at turnabout. They believe in the winning horse; they will wear anybody's coat who may choose to give them one. They are to be bought by the dozen, like mackerel, but he who gives a penny for them wastes his money. Profit is their god, and whether they make it out of you or your enemy, the money is just as sweet to them. Heads or tails are alike to them so long as they win. High road or back lane, all's the same to them so that they can get home with the loaf in the basket. They are friends to the goose but they will eat his giblets. So long as the water turns their wheel, it is none the worse for being muddy. They never lose a chance of minding the main chance.

Others are shifty because they are so desperately fond of good fellowship. "Hail fellow, well met," is their cry, be it traveler or highwayman. They are so good-natured that they must needs agree with everybody. They are cousins of Mr. Anything. Their brains are in other people's heads. They are mere time-servers, in hopes that the times may serve them. They belong to the party which wears the yellow colors, not in their button-holes, but in the palms of their hands. Butter them, and like turnips you may eat them. Pull the rope, and like the bells they will ring as you choose to make them, funeral knell or wedding peal. They have no backbones; you may bend them like willow wands, backward or forward, whichever way you please. Like oysters, anybody may pepper them who can open them. Sweet to you and sweet to your enemy. They blow hot and cold. They try to be Jack-o'-both sides, and deserve to be kicked like a football by both parties.

Some are hypocrites by nature; slippery as eels, and piebald like Squire Smoothey's mare. Like a drunken man, they could not walk straight if they were to try. Like corn-dealers, they are rogues ingrain. They were born of the breed of St. Judas. The double shuffle is their favorite game, and honesty their greatest hatred. Honey is on their tongue, but gall in their hearts. They are mongrel bred, like the gypsy's dog. Like a cat's feet they show soft pads, but carry sharp claws. If speaking the truth and lying were equally profitable, they would naturally prefer to lie, for, like dirt to a pig, it would be congenial. They fawn, and flatter, and cringe, and scrape. Like snails they make their way by their slime; but all the while they hate you in their hearts, and only wait for a chance to stab you. Beware of those who come from the town of Deceit. Mr. Facing-both-ways, Mr. Fair-speech, and Mr. Two-tongues are neighbors who are best at a distance. Though they look one way, as boatmen do, they are pulling the other; they are false as the Devil's promises, and as cruel as death and the grave.

Religious deceivers are the worst, I fear they are as plentiful as rats in an old wheatstack. They cover up their black flesh with white feathers. Saturday and Sunday make a wonderful difference. They have the fear of the minister a deal more before their eyes than the fear of God. Their religion lies in imitating the religious; they have none of the root of the matter in them. They carry Dr. Watts' hymnbook in their pocket, and sing a roaring song at the same time. Their Sunday coats are the best part about them. They prate like parrots, but their talk and their walk do not agree. Some of them are fishing for customers, and a little pious talk is a cheap advertisement. If the seat at the church or the meeting costs a trifle, they make it up out of short weights. They do not worship God while they trade, but they trade on their worship. Others of the poorer sort go to church for soup, and bread, and coal tickets. They love the communion because of the alms' money. Some of the dear old Mrs. Goodbodies want a blessed almshouse, and so they profess to be so blessed under the blessed ministry of their blessed pastor every blessed Sunday. Charity suits them if faith does not; they know which side their bread is buttered on.

Others make a decent show in religion to quiet their consciences; they use it as a salve for their wounds. If they could satisfy Heaven as easily as they quiet themselves it would be a fine thing for them. I have met with some who went a long way in profession, as far as I could see, for nothing but the love of being thought a deal of. They got a little knot of friends to believe in their fine talk, and take all in for gospel that they liked to say. Their opinion was the true measure of a preacher's soundness; they could settle up everything by their own know. They had experience for those who liked something hot and strong; but dear, dear, if they had but condescended to show a little Christian practice as well, how much better their lives would have been! These people are like owls, which look to be big birds, but they are not, for they are all feathers; they look wonderfully knowing in the twilight, but when the light comes they are regular boobies.

Hypocrites of all sorts are abominable. He who deals with them will be sorry for it. He who tries to cheat the Lord will be quite ready to cheat his fellow men. Great cry generally means little wool. Many a big fireplace in which you expect to see bacon and hams, when you look up, has nothing to show you but its empty hooks and black soot. Some men's windmills are only nut-crackers—their elephants are nothing but baby pigs. It is not all who go to church or meeting that truly pray, nor those who sing loudest that praise God most, nor those who pull the longest faces who are the most in earnest.

What mean animals hypocrites must be! talk of weasels, they are nothing to them. Better be a dead dog than a live hypocrite. Surely when the Devil sees hypocrites at their little game, it must be as good as a play to him. He tempts genuine Christians, but he lets these alone, because he is sure of them.

Depend upon it, friends, if a straight line will not pay, a crooked one will not. What is got by shuffling is very dangerous gain. It may give a moment's peace to wear a mask, but deception will come home to you and bring sorrow with it. Honesty is the best policy. If the lion's skin does not do, never try the fox's. Be as true as steel. Let your face and hands, like the church clock, always tell how your inner works are going. Better be laughed at as Tom Tell-truth than be praised as Crafty Charlie. Plain dealing may bring us trouble, but it is better than shuffling. At the last the upright will have their reward, but for the double-minded to get to Heaven is as impossible as for a man to swim across the Atlantic with a mill-stone under each arm.

Hints as to Thriving

HARD WORK is the grand secret of success. Nothing but rags and poverty can come of idleness. Elbow grease is the only stuff to make gold with. No sweat, no sweet. He who would have the crow's eggs must climb the tree. Every man must build up his own fortune. Shirt sleeves rolled up lead on to best broadcloth. He who is not ashamed of the apron will soon be able to do without it. "Diligence is the mother of good luck," as poor Richard says; but "Idleness is the Devil's bolster," as John Ploughman says.

Believe in traveling on step by step; do not expect to be rich in a jump.

> Great greediness to reap
> Helps not the money heap.

Slow and sure is better than fast and flimsy. Perseverance, by its daily gains, enriches a man far more than fits and starts of fortunate speculation. Little fishes are sweet. Every little helps, as the sow said when she snapped at a gnat. Every day a thread makes a skein in a year. Brick by brick houses are built. We should creep before we walk, walk before we run, and run before we ride. In getting rich the more haste the worse speed. Haste trips up its own heels. Hasty climbers have sudden falls.

It is bad beginning business without capital. It is hard marketing with empty pockets. We want a nest egg, for hens will lay where there are eggs already. It is true you must bake with the flour you have, but if the sack is empty it might be well not to set up for a baker. Making bricks without straw is easy enough compared with making money when you have none to start with. You, young gentleman, stay as an apprentice a little longer, till you have saved; fly when your wings have got feathers. If you try it too soon you will be like the young rook that broke its neck through trying to fly before it was fledged. Every minnow wants to be a whale, but it is prudent to be a little fish while you have but little water; when your pond becomes the sea, then swell as much as you like. Trading without capital is like building a house without bricks, making a fire without sticks, burning candles without wicks; it leads men into tricks, and lands them in a fix.

Do not give up a small business till you see that a large one will pay you better. Even crumbs are bread.

> Better a poor horse than an empty stall;
> Better half a loaf than none at all.

Better a little furniture than an empty house. In these hard times he who can sit on a stone and feed himself had better not move. From bad to worse is poor improvement. A crust is hard fare, but none at all is harder. Do not jump out of the frying pain into the fire. Remember, many men have done well in very small shops. A little trade with profit is better than a great concern at a loss. A small fire that warms you is better than a large fire that burns you. A great deal of water can be got from a small pipe if the bucket is always there to catch it. Large hares may be caught in small woods. A sheep may get fat in a small meadow, and starve in a great desert. He who undertakes too much succeeds but little. Two shops are like two stools, a man comes to the ground

HINTS AS TO THRIVING

between them. You may burst a bag by trying to fill it too full, and ruin yourself by grasping at too much.

> In a great river great fish are found,
> But take good heed lest you be drown'd.

Make as few changes as you can; trees often transplanted bear little fruit. If you have difficulties in one place you will have them in another. If you move because it is damp in the valley, you may find it cold on the hill. Where will the ass go that he will not have to work? Where can a cow live and not get milked? Where will you find land without stones, or meat without bones? Everywhere on earth men must eat bread in the sweat of their faces. To fly from trouble men must have eagles' wings. Alteration is not always improvement, as the pigeon said when she got out of the net and into the pie. There is a proper time for changing, and then mind you bestir yourself, for a sitting hen gets no barley. Do not be forever on the shift for a rolling stone gathers no moss. Stick-to-it is the conqueror. He who can wait long enough will win. This, that, and the other, anything, and everything, all put together make nothing in the end; but on one horse a man rides home in due season. In one place the seed grows, in one nest the bird hatches its eggs, in one oven the bread bakes, in one river the fish lives.

Do not be above your business. He who turns up his nose at his work quarrels with his bread and butter. He is a poor smith who is afraid of his own sparks; there's some discomfort in all trades except chimney-sweeping. If sailors gave up going to sea because of the wet; if bakers left off baking because it is hot work; if plowmen would not plow because of the cold, and tailors would not make clothes for fear of pricking their fingers, what a pass we should come to! Nonesense, my fine fellow, there is no shame about any honest calling; do not be afraid of soiling your hands, there is plenty of soap to be had. All trades are good to good traders. A clever man can make money out of dirt. Lucifer matches pay well if you sell enough of them.

You cannot get honey if you are frightened at bees, nor sow corn if you are afraid of getting mud on your boots. Lackadaisical gentlemen had better emigrate to Fool's-land, where men get their living by wearing shiny boots and gloves. When bars of iron melt under the south wind, when you can dig the fields with tooth-picks, blow ships along with fans, manure the crops with lavender water, and grow plumcake in flowerpots, then will be a fine time for dandies. Until the millennium comes we shall all have a deal to put up with, and had better bear our present burdens than run helter-skelter where we shall find matters a deal worse.

Plod is the word. Every one must row with such oars as he has, and as he cannot choose the wind, he must sail by such as God sends him. Patience and attention will get on in the long run. If the cat sits long enough at the hole she will catch the mouse. Always-at-it grows good cabbage and lettuce where others grow thistles. I know as a plowman that it is up and down, up and down the field that plows the acres; there's no getting over the ground a mile at a time.

Keep your weather eye open. Sleeping poultry are carried off by the fox. Who watches not catches not. Fools ask what is the time, but wise men know their time. Grind while the wind blows, or if not do not blame providence. God sends every bird its food, but He does not throw it into the nest: He gives us our daily bread, but it is through our own labor. Take time by the forelock. Be up early and catch the worm. The morning hour carries gold in its mouth. He who drives last in the row gets all the dust in his eyes. Rise early, and you will have a clear start for the day.

Never try dirty dodges to make money. It will never pay you to lick honey off of thorns. An honest man will not make a dog of himself for the sake of getting a bone. It is hard to walk on the Devil's ice; it is fine skating, but it ends in a heavy fall, and worse. He needs have a long spoon who would eat out of the same dish with Satan. Never ruin your soul for the sake of pelf: it is like drowning yourself in a well to get a drink of water. Take nothing in hand that may bring you repentance. Better walk barefoot than ride in a carriage to Hell; better that the bird starve than be fattened for the spit. The mouse wins little by nibbling the cheese if it gets caught in the trap. Clean money or none, mark that; for gain badly gotten will be an everlasting loss.

A good article, full weight, and a fair price bring customers to the shop, but people do not recommend the shop where they are cheated. Cheats never thrive; or if they do it must be in the big city, where they catch chance customers enough to live by. A rogue's purse is full of holes. He will have blisters on his feet who wears stolen shoes. He whose fingers are like lime-twigs will find other things stick to them besides silver. Steal eels and they will turn to snakes. The more a fox robs the sooner he will be hunted. If a rogue wants to make a good trade he had better turn honest. If all you aim at is profit, still deal uprightly, for it is the most paying game.

Look most to your spending. No matter what comes in, if more goes out you will always be poor. The art is not in making money, but in keeping it. Little expenses, like mice in a barn, when they are many, make great waste. Hair by hair heads get bald. Straw by straw the thatch goes off the cottage, and drop by drop the rain comes into the room. A barrel is soon empty if the tap leaks but a drop a minute. Chickens will be plucked feather by feather if the maid keeps at it; small mites eat the cheese; little birds destroy a great deal of wheat. When you mean to save, begin with your mouth; there are many thieves down the red lane. The ale jug is a great waster. In all other things keep within compass. In clothes choose suitable and lasting stuff, and not tawdry fineries. Never stretch your legs farther than your blankets will reach, or you will soon be cold. A fool may make money, but it needs a wise man to spend it. Remember it is easier to build two chimneys than to keep one going. If you give all to back and board there is nothing left for the savings bank. Fare hard and work hard while you are young, and you have a chance of rest when you are old.

Never indulge in extravangance unless you want to make a short cut to the poorhouse. Money has wings of its own, and if you find it another pair of wings, wonder not if it flies fast.

> He that hath it, and will not keep it;
> He that wants it, and will not seek it;
> He that drinks and is not dry,
> Shall want money as well as I.

If many poor people could only see the amount of money which they melt away in drink their hair would stand on end with fright. We should need to get up earlier in the morning to spend all our money, because we should find ourselves suddenly made quite rich through stopping the drip of the tap. At any rate, you young people who want to get on in the world must make a point of settling in

HINTS AS TO THRIVING

your spirits that no spirits shall ever settle you. Have your luxuries, if you must have them, after you have made your fortunes, but just now look after your bread and cheese.

My talk seems like the Irishman's rope which he could not get into the ship because somebody had cut the end off. I only want to say, do not be greedy, for covetousness is always poor. Strive to get on, for poverty is no virtue, and to rise in the world is to a man's credit as well as his comfort. Earn all you can, save all you can, and then give all you can. Never try to save out of God's cause; such money will canker the rest. Giving to God is no loss; it is putting your substance into the best bank. Giving is true having, as the old gravestone said: "What I spent I had, what I saved I lost, what I gave I have." The pockets of the poor are safe lockers, and it is always a good investment to lend to the Lord. John Ploughman wishes all young beginners long life and prosperity.

> Sufficient of wealth,
> And abundant health,
> Long years of content,
> And when life is spent
> A mansion with God in glory.

Tall Talk

THE ART OF STRETCHING is uncommonly general. Gooseberries are to be heard of weighing twice as much as possible, and unseen showers of frogs fall regularly when newspapers are slack. If a cart goes by and rattles the lid of an old woman's teapot, it is put down as an earthquake. Fine imaginations are not at all scarce. Certain people are always on the lookout for wonders, and if they do not see them they invent them. They see comets every night, and hear some rare tale every day. All their molehills are mountains. All their ducks are swans. They have learned the multiplication table, and use it freely. If they saw six dogs together they would swear they saw a hundred hounds; yes, and get as red in the face as turkey-cocks if anybody looked a little doubtful. Before long they would persuade themselves that they saw ten thousand lions; for everything grows with them as fast as mushrooms.

All things around them are wonderful, but as for themselves, nobody is fit to clean their shoes. They are the cream of creation. They are as strong as Samson, and could pull against John Ploughman's team, only they will not try it, for fear of hurting the horses. Their wealth is enormous; they *could* pay off the national debt, only they have good reasons for not doing so just yet. If they keep shop they turn over several millions in the year, and only stop in business at all for the sake of their neighbors. They sell the best goods at the lowest

TALL TALK

prices, in fact, under cost price. None in the country are fit to hold a candle to them. If they take a farm it is only for amusement, and to show the poor natives how to do it. All their doings are wonders! Like the wild beast show which stopped at our village, they are *the only, original, and unrivaled!* But they are quite as dead a sell as that fine affair was. All the best of it was outside on the pictures, and it's just the same with them. How they do draw the long bow! Hear them talk. It is all in capital letters and notes of admiration. "Did you ever see SUCH A HORSE? Why sir, it would beat the wind!! THAT COW—let me call your attention to her, there is not such another in the county; JUST NOTICE THE SWING OF HER TAIL!! Yes, sir, THAT BOY of mine *is* intelligent, far beyond his years. He's a perfect prodigy! *Like his father,* did you say? Very kind remark, but there's a good deal of truth in it. Though I say it, a man must get up early to beat ME! *I'm one too many for most people!* Just look over the farm. Was there ever such A FIELD OF TURNIPS, with ventilated leaves pricked through by nature to let the air in and out! Too many moles did you say? Ah! thereby hangs a tale. Do you know OUR MOLES throw up bigger hills than any others, and are supposed to be of a FINE OLD STOCK now almost lost. Did you notice that TREMENDOUS THISTLE? Is it not a rare specimen? enough to make a Scotchman die of joy. That shows the EXTRAORDINARY richness of the soil; and, indeed, sir, OUR LAST YEAR'S CROP OF WHEAT was so amazingly heavy, I thought we should never get it home. It nearly broke the wagons; we had half the county here to see it threshed, and the oldest men in the parish said they never heard tell of the like. IT IS A MERCY THAT STEAM IS INVENTED, OR WE NEVER COULD HAVE THRESHED IT BY HAND."

When a man gets into this style of talk, it is no matter

what he is hammering at, he speaks of it as the finest, greatest, and most marvelous in the kingdom, or else the most awful, horrible, and dreadful in the world. His boots would not fit Goliath, but his tongue is much too big for the giant's mouth. He paints with a broom. He sugars his dumpling with a spade, and lays on his butter with a trowel. *His* horse, *his* dog, *his* gun, *his* wife, *his* child, *his* singing, *his* planning, are all nonesuches, he lives at Number One, and it would be hard to find a man fit to be number two to him. The water out of his well is stronger than wine; it rains pea-soup into his water butt; his currant bushes grow grapes; you might live inside one of his pumpkins. His flowers—well, he's heard that the Queen herself had a fellow plant to that geranium, only his was the better! The greatest wonder is that men of this type do not see that everybody is laughing at them; they must have bragged themselves blind. Everybody sees the bottom of their dish, and yet they go on calling it an ocean, as if they had none but flat fish to deal with.

I have known men who open their mouths like barn doors in boasting what they would do *if* they were in somebody else's shoes. They would abolish all taxes, turn poorhouses into palaces, make the pumps run with liquor, and set the place on fire; but all this depends on an *if*, and that *if* is a sort of five-barred gate which they have never got over. If the sky falls we shall catch larks. If Jack Brag does but get the reins he will make the horses fly up to the moon. *If* is a fine word; when a man jumps on its back it will carry him into worlds which were never created, and make him see miracles which were never wrought. With an *if* you may put a city into a quart pot.

TALL TALK

> If all the seas were one sea,
> What a great sea that would be!
> And if all the trees were one tree,
> What a great tree that would be!
> And if all the axes were one axe,
> What a great axe that would be!
> And if all the men were one man,
> What a great man he would be!
> And if the great man took the great axe,
> And cut down the great tree,
> And let it fall into the great sea,
> What a splish splash that would be!

"What nonsense!" says someone; so John Ploughman thinks. Therefore he puts it in as a specimen of the stupidity which tall talkers are so fond of. This is not half so silly as nine out of ten of their mighty nothings.

What some of these fellows have done! Now, would you believe it? (I say, "No, I would not.") They made their own fortunes in no time, and made other people's too. Their advice has been the means of filling many a bag with gold. What they said at a meeting fastened the people to their seats like cobbler's wax. They were in a quarrel, and when all their party were nearly beaten, they settled off the opposition side at once with first-rate wit and wisdom—King Solomon was a fool to them. As to religion, they were the first to set it up in the parish. By their wonderful exertions everything was set a going. People are not grateful, or they would almost worship them: it's shameful to see how they have been neglected, and even turned off, of late by the very people whom they have been the making of. While they had a finger in the pie all went well at the meeting, but now they have left they say there's a screw loose, and they who live longest will see most. When they are in a modest humor they borrow words from David, and say, "The earth is dissolved, I bear up the pillars of it." It is thought that their death would fill the world with bones. If they remove their trade people are expected to shut up their shops directly. It is only the shopkeeper's impudence that makes them hope to get a living after such customers are gone. When they feel a little natural pride at their great doings, then it is fine to hear them go ahead. Talk of blowing your own trumpet, they have a whole band of music, big drum and all, and keep all the instruments going to their own praise and glory.

I would rather plow all day and be on the road with the wagon all night when it freezes your eyelashes than listen to these great talkers. I'd sooner go without eating till I was lean than eat the best turkey that ever came on the table, and be dinned all the while with their jaw. They talk on such a mighty scale, and magnify everything so thunderingly, that you cannot believe them when they accidentally slip in a word or two of truth. You are apt to think that even their cheese is chalk. They are great liars, but they are hardly conscious of it; they have talked themselves into believing their own bombast. The frog thought herself equal to the cow, and then began to blow herself out to make it true. They swell like her and they will burst like her if they do not take care.

Everybody who knows big talkers should take warning from them:

> Said I to myself, here's a lesson for me,
> This man is a picture of what I might be.

We must try to state the truth, the whole truth, and nothing but the truth. If we begin calling eleven inches a foot we shall go on till we call one inch four-and-twenty. If we call a heifer a cow, we may one day call a dormouse

TALL TALK

a bullock. Once go in for exaggeration, and you may as well be hung for a sheep as a lamb. You have left the road of truth, and there is no telling where the crooked lane may lead you. He who tells little lies will soon think nothing of great ones, for the principle is the same. Where there is a mousehole there will soon be a rathole, and if the kitten comes the cat will follow. It seldom rains but it pours; a little untruth leads on to a perfect shower of lying.

Self-praise is no recommendation. A man's praise smells sweet when it comes out of other men's mouths. Grow your own cherries, but don't sing your own praises.

Boasters are never worth a button with the shank off. Long tongue, short hand. Great talkers, little doers. Dogs that bark much run away when it is time to bite. The leanest pig squeaks most. It is not the hen which cackles most that lays most eggs. Saying and doing are two different things. It is the barren cow that bellows. There may be great noise of threshing where there is no wheat. Great boast, little roast. Drums sound loud because there is nothing in them. Good men know themselves too well to chant their own praises. Barges without cargoes float high on the canal, but the fuller they are the lower they sink. Good cheese sells itself without puffery. When men are really excellent, people find it out. Bounce is the sign of folly. Loud braying reveals an ass. If a man is ignorant and holds his tongue, no one will despise him. If he rattles on with an empty pate, and a tongue that brags like forty, he will write out his own name in capital letters. They will be: **F O O L.**

As "by the ears the ass is known"—
A truth as sure as parsons preach,
"The man," as proverbs long have shown,
"Is seen most plainly through his speech."

Things I Would Not Choose

IF IT WERE ALL THE SAME to other folks, and I might have things managed exactly as I liked, I should not choose to have my book pulled to pieces by fellows who have not the honesty to read it, but make up their minds beforehand, as Simple Simon did when they put him on the jury. However, if it amuses others to find fault with me, they are as welcome as they are free. The anvil is not afraid of the hammer. They tell me editors cut a page open, and then smell the knife, and fall to praising the book up to the skies, or abusing it without mercy, according as the maggot bites them, or according to what they have had for dinner. John Ploughman hopes the publisher will turn down this leaf when he sends his book to the printers, and he hopes the following word to the wise will be enough: *I hope my pears will not fall into pigs' mouths.*

I should not choose, if I might have my own way, to see a dozen of these pages brought home wrapped round the butter the next time we send to the shop. It is not at all unlikely to happen, so I must put up with it, as Tom Higgs did when he had only turkey and plum pudding for dinner.

I should not choose to plow with two old horses spavined and broken-winded, and altogether past work. Pity the poor horses and pity the poor plowman, and no pity at all for the farmer who keeps such cattle. When I see a man whipping and slashing a poor horse, I want to

THINGS I WOULD NOT CHOOSE

kick him. At the same time I feel glad that my Violet and Dapper go well enough with the sound of the whip without needing to be paid like lawyers for all they do. A man who knocks a horse about ought to be put in harness himself. There is a deal to be done with animals with kindness, and nothing with cruelty. He who is unmerciful to his beast is worse than the beast.

I should not choose to be a bob-tailed cow in summer, nor a servant with a score of masters, nor a minister with half-a-dozen tyrants for deacons. Nor should I like to try the truth of the old saying—

> Two cats and one mouse,
> Two women in one house,
> Two dogs to one bone,
> Will not agree long.

I had rather not be a dog with a tin kettle tied to his tail, nor a worm on a fisherman's hook, nor an eel being skinned alive, nor a husband with a vixen for his wife. I would much rather not fall into the jaws of a crocodile or the hands of a lawyer. The only suit that lasts too long is a lawsuit, and that would not suit me at all. I would not choose to be gossiped to death by washerwomen, or pestered by a traveling bookseller wanting me to take in series numbers of a book that will run on forever like old Jimmy's debts.

I should be very hard up before I should choose to sleep with pigs, or live in some people's dirty houses. I would not choose to own half the cottages poor laborers are made to live in. No farmer would be so mean as to keep his horses in them, and they are not good enough for dog kennels. Think of father, and mother, and a son, and two daughters sleeping in the same room! It is a burning shame, and a crying sin on the part of those who drive people to such shifts. If any man defends such a system, half-an-hour's hanging would be a good thing.

To be servant to a miser, to work for a wasp, to be catspaw to a monkey, or toady to a superior without brains, I would not choose. I would not go round with the hat for my own pocket, nor borrow money, nor be a loafer, nor live like a toad under a harrow, no, not for all that ever thawed out of the cold hand of charity.

Bad off as I am, I would not choose to change, unless I could hope to better myself. Who would go under the waterspout to get out of the rain? What's the use of traveling to the other end of the world to be worse off than you are? Botany Bay for those who like to transport themselves.

I would not choose to drive a pig, nor to manage a jibbing horse, nor try to persuade a man with a wooden head. I should not like to be a schoolmaster with unruly boys, nor a bull baited by dogs, nor a hen who has hatched ducks. Worse off still is a preacher to drowsy hearers; he hunts with dead dogs and drives wooden horses. As well hold a service for sleeping swine as sleeping men.

I would not buy a horse of a horsedealer if I could help it. A very honest horsedealer will never cheat you if you do not let him; an ordinary one will draw your eyetooth while your mouth is shut. Horses are almost as hard to judge as men's hearts; the oldest judges are taken in. What with bone-spavin, ringbone and splints; grease, crown-scab and rat-tail, wind-galls and cankers, colic and jaundice, sandcracks and founders, mallenders and sallenders, there is hardly a sound horse. It's a bad thing to change horses at all; if you have a good one keep it, for you will not get a better; if you have a bad one keep it, for ten to one you will buy a worse one.

THINGS I WOULD NOT CHOOSE

I would not choose to make myself a doormat nor a poodle, nor a fellow who will eat dirt in order to curry favor with great folks. Let who will tell lies to please others, I would rather have truth on my side, if I go barefoot. Independence and a clear conscience are better with cold cabbage than slavery and sin with roast beef.

I would not like to keep a tollgate at the top of a long hill, nor to be a tax collector, nor the summoning officer, nor a general nuisance, nor a poor postman with half enough to live on; better be a gypsy's horse, and live on the common, with no hay and no oats, but plenty of oak cudgel.

I would not choose to be plucked like a goose, nor to be shareholder in a company; nor to be fried alive.

I would not stand as godfather to anybody's child, to promise that the little sinner shall keep God's holy commandments and walk in the same all the days of his life. Of the two, I would sooner promise to put the moon into my coat sleeve and bring it out again at the leg of my trousers, or vow that the little dear shall have red hair and a snub nose. Neither would I choose to have lies told over my baby in the hope of getting on the pastor's blind side when the blankets were given away at Christmas.

I would not choose to go where I should be afraid to die, nor could I bear to live without a good hope for the hereafter. I would not choose to sit on a barrel of gunpowder and smoke a pipe. That is what those do who are thoughtless about their souls while life is so uncertain. Neither would I choose my lot on earth, but leave it with God to choose for me. I might pick and choose and take the worst, but His choice is always best.

Try

OF ALL THE PRETTY LITTLE SONGS I have ever heard my youngsters sing, one of the best is—

>If at first you don't succeed,
>Try, try, try again.

I recommend it to grown up people who are down in the mouth, and fancy that the best thing they can do is to give up. Nobody knows what he can do till he tries. "We shall get through it now," said Jack to Harry as they finished up the pudding. Everything new is hard work, but a little of the "try" ointment rubbed on the hand and worked into the heart makes things easy.

Can't do it sticks in the mud, but *Try* soon drags the wagon out of the rut. The fox said Try, and he got away from the hounds when they almost snapped at him. The bees said Try, and turned flowers into honey. The squirrel said Try, and up he went to the top of the beech tree. The snowdrop said Try, and bloomed in the cold snows of winter. The sun said Try, and the spring soon threw Jack Frost out of the saddle. The young lark said Try, and he found that his new wings took him over hedges and ditches, and up where his father was singing. The ox said Try, and plowed the field from end to end. No hill too steep for Try to climb, no clay too stiff for Try to plow, no field too wet for Try to drain, no hole too big for Try to mend.

TRY

> By little strokes
> Men fell great oaks.

By a spadeful at a time navvies digged, cut a big hole through the hill, and heaped up the embankment.

> The stone is hard, and the drop is small,
> But a hole is made by the constant fall.

What man has done man can do, and what has never been may be. Plowmen have gotten to be gentlemen, cobblers have turned their lapstones into gold, and tailors have sprouted into Members of Parliament. Roll up your shirt sleeves, young Hopeful, and go at it. Where there is a will there's a way. The sun shines for all the world. Believe in God, and work hard, and see if the mountains are not removed. Faint heart never won fair lady. God helps those who help themselves. Never mind luck, that's what the fool had when he killed himself with eating suet pudding; the best luck in all the world is made up of joint oil and sticking plaster.

Do not wait for helpers. Try those two old friends, your strong arms. If the fox wants poultry for his cubs he must carry the chickens home himself. None of her friends can help the hare; she must run for herself, or the greyhounds will have her. Every man must carry his own sack to the mill. You must put your own shoulder to the wheel and keep it there, for there's plenty of ruts in the road. If you wait till all the ways are paved, you will have light shining between your ribs. If you sit still till great men take you on their backs, you will grow to your seat. Your own legs are better than stilts; don't look to others, but trust in God and keep your powder dry.

Do not be whining about not having a fair start. Throw a sensible man out of a window, he will fall on his legs and ask the nearest way to his work. The more you have to begin with the less you will have at the end. Money you earn yourself is much brighter and sweeter than any you get out of dead men's bags. A scant breakfast in the morning of life whets the appetite for a feast later in the day. He who has tasted a sour apple will have the more relish for a sweet one. Your present want will make future prosperity all the sweeter. Small money has set up many a peddler in business, and he has turned it over till he has his carriage.

As for the place you are cast in, do not find fault with that. You need not be a horse because you were born in a stable. If a bull tossed a man of mettle sky high he would drop down into a good place. A hard-working young man, with his wits about him, will make money where others do nothing but lose it.

> Who loves his work and knows to spare,
> May live and flourish anywhere.

As to a little trouble, who expects to find cherries without stones, or roses without thorns? Who would win must learn to bear. Idleness lies in bed sick of the mulligrubs. Industry finds health and wealth. The dog in the kennel barks at the fleas; the hunting dog does not even know they are there. Laziness waits till the river is dry and never gets to market; "Try" swims it and makes all the trade. Cannot do it could not eat the bread and butter which was cut for him, but Try made meat out of mushrooms.

Everybody who does not get on blames it all on competition. When the wine was stolen they said it was the rats; it is very convenient to have a horse to put the saddle on. A mouse may find a hole, be the room ever so full of cats. Good workmen are always wanted. No barber ever shaves so close but another barber will find something left. Nothing is so good but what it might be better; and he who sells the best wins the trade. We were all going to the poorhouse because of the new machines, so the prophets were always telling us. Instead of it, all these threshing, and reaping, and haying machines have helped to make those men better off who had sense enough to work them. If a man has not a soul above clodhopping he may expect to keep poor, but if he opens his sense-box, and picks up here a little and there a little, even Johnny Raw may yet improve. "Times are bad," they say. Yes, and if you go gaping about and send your wits wool gathering, times always will be bad.

Many do not get on because they have not the pluck to begin in right earnest. The first money laid by is the difficulty. The first blow is half the battle. Up with the "Try" flag, then out to your work and away to the bank with the savings, and you will be a man yet. Poor men will always be poor if they think they must be. But there is a way up out of the lowest poverty if a man looks after it early, before he has a wife and half-a-dozen children. After that he carries too much weight for racing, and most commonly he must be content if he finds bread for the hungry mouths and clothes for the little backs. Yet, I don't know; some hens scratch all the better for having a swarm of chicks. To young men the road up the hill may be hard, but at any rate it is open, and they who set stout heart against a stiff hill shall climb it yet. What was hard to bear will be sweet to remember. If young men would deny themselves, work hard, live hard, and save in their early days, they need not keep their noses to the grindstone all their lives, as many do. Let them be teetotalers; water is the strongest drink, it drives mills. It's the drink of lions and horses, and Samson never drank anything else.

If you want to do good in the world, the little word "Try" comes in. There are plenty of ways of serving God, and some that will fit you exactly as a key fits a lock. Do not hold back because you cannot preach in a large church; be content to talk to one or two in a cottage; very good wheat grows in little fields. You may cook in small pots as well as in big ones. Little pigeons can carry great messages. Even a little dog can bark at a thief, and wake up the master and save the house. A spark is fire. A sentence of truth has Heaven in it. Do what you do right thoroughly, pray over it heartily, and leave the result to God.

Alas! advice is thrown away on many, like good seed on a bare rock. Teach a cow for seven years, but she will never learn to sing the Old Hundredth. Of some it seems true that when they were born Solomon went by the door, but would not look in. Their coat of arms is a fool's cap. They sleep when it is time to plow, and weep when harvest comes. They eat all the parsnips for supper, and wonder they have none left for breakfast. Our working people are shamefully unthrifty, and so the world swarms with poor. If what is spent in waste were only saved against a rainy day, poorhouses would never be built.

> Once let every man say *Try*,
> Very few on straw would lie,
> Fewer still of want would die;
> Pans would all have fish to fry;
> Pigs would fill the poor man's sty;
> Want would cease and need would fly;
> Wives and children cease to cry;
> Poor rates would not swell so high;
> Things wouldn't go so much awry—
> You'd be glad, and so would I.

Monuments

EVERY MAN SHOULD LEAVE a monument behind him in recollection of his own life by his neighbors. There must be something very much amiss about a man who is not missed when he dies. A good character is the best tombstone. Those who loved you, and were helped by you, will remember you when forget-me-nots are withered. Carve your name on hearts, and not on marble. So live toward others that they will keep your memory green when the grass grows on your grave. Let us hope there will be something better to be said about us than of the man whose epitaph is here:

> Here lies a man who did no good,
> And if he'd lived he never would;
> Where he's gone, and how he fares,
> Nobody knows and nobody cares.

May our friends never remember us as great gormandisers of meat and drink, like the glutton over whose grave is written:

> Gentle reader, gentle reader,
> Look on the spot where I do lie,
> I always was a very good feeder,
> But now the worms do feed on I.

As much as that might be said of a prize fat bullock, if it died of disease.

However, a plain-speaking tombstone is better than

downright lying. To put flattery on a grave is like pouring melted butter down a stone sink.

Where do they bury the bad people? Right and left in our churchyard. They seem all to have been the best of folks, a regular nest of saints; and some of them so precious good, it is no wonder they died—they were too fine to live in such a wicked world as this. Better give bread to the poor than stones to the dead. Better kind words to the living than fine speeches over the grave. Some of the things said on monuments is enough to make a dead man blush.

What heaps of marble are put over many big people's tombs! Half enough to build a house with! What a lift they will have at the resurrection! It makes me feel as if I could not get my breath to think of all those stones being heaped on my bones. Let the earth which I have turned over so often lie light upon me when it is turned over me. Let John Ploughman be buried somewhere under the boughs of a spreading beech, with a green grass mound above him, out of which primroses and daises peep in their season; a quiet shady spot where the leaves fall, and the robins play, and the dewdrops gleam in the sunshine. Let the wind blow fresh and free over me, and if there must be a line about me, let it be:

HERE LIES THE BODY OF
JOHN PLOUGHMAN,
WAITING FOR THE APPEARING OF HIS
LORD AND SAVIOUR,
JESUS CHRIST.

I have often heard tell of patience on a monument, but I have never seen it sitting there when I have gone through churchyards. I have a good many times seen stupidity on a monument, and I have wondered why the

MONUMENTS

parson, or the churchwarden, or whoever else has the ruling of things, let people cut such rubbish on the stones.

I have read pretty near enough silly things myself in our burying-grounds to fill a book. Better leave the grave alone than set up a monument to ignorance.

Of all places for jokes and fun the queerest are tombstones, yet many a time gravestones have had such oddities carved upon them that one is led to think, the nearer the church the further from common decency.

Why could not people poke fun somewhere else? A man's wit must be nearly dead when he can find no place for it but the graveyard. The body of the raggedest beggar is too sacred a thing to crack jokes upon.

There is proof positive that some fools are left alive to to write on the monuments of those who are buried. I say let us have a law to let nobody put nonsense over the dead unless to take out a certificate. At the same time, let all flattery be saved for dry goods shops and quack doctors, and none be allowed at the grave. I say as our minister does—

> Let no proud stone with sculptur'd virtues rise,
> To mark the spot wherein a sinner lies,
> Or if some boast must deck the sinner's grave,
> Boast of His love who died lost man to save.

One more, and John Ploughman leaves the churchyard to go about his work.

> Like to the damask rose you see,
> Or like the blossom on the tree,
> Or like the dainty flow'r of May,
> Or like the morning of the day,
> Or like the sun, or like the shade,
> Or like the gourd which Jonah had;
> Even so is man, whose thread is spun,
> Drawn out, and cut, and so is done:

The rose withers, the blossom blasteth,
The flower fades, the morning hasteth,
The sun sets, the shadow flies,
The gourd consumes, and man he dies.

Very Ignorant People

I KNOW A GOOD MANY who certainly could not tell what great A or little A may mean; but some of these people are not the most ignorant in the world for all that. For instance, they know a cow's head from its tail, and one of the election gentlemen said lately that the candidate did not know that. They know that turnips do not grow on trees, and they can tell a mangold-wurtzel from a beet root, and a rabbit from a hare, and there are fine folk who play on pianos who hardly know as much as that. If they cannot read they can plow, and mow, and reap, and sow, and bring up seven children and yet pay their way; and there's a sight of people who are much too ignorant to do that. Ignorance of spelling books is very bad, but ignorance of hard work is worse. Wisdom does not always speak Latin. If no ignorant people ate bread but those who wear hobnail shoes, corn would be a deal cheaper. Wisdom in a poor man is like a diamond set in lead, for none but good judges can discover its value. Wisdom walks often in patched clothes, and then folks do not admire her. But I say, never mind the coat, give me the man: shells are nothing, the kernel is everything.

I would have everybody able to read and write, and figure; indeed, I don't think a man can know too much; but mark you, the knowing of these things is not education. There are millions of your reading and writing people who are as ignorant as neighbor Norton's calf, that did not know its own mother. To know how to read and write is like having tools to work with, but if you do not use these tools, and your eyes, and your ears too, you will be none the better off. Everybody should know what most concerns him and makes him most useful. If cats can catch mice and hens can lay eggs, they know the things which most suits what they were made for. It is little use for a horse to know how to fly, it will do well enough if it can trot. A man on a farm ought to learn what belongs to farming, a blacksmith should study a horse's foot, a dairymaid should be well up in skimming the milk and making the butter, and a laborer's wife should be a good scholar in the sciences of boiling and baking, washing and mending. John Ploughman ventures to say that those men and women who have not learned the duties of their callings are very ignorant people, even if they can give the Greek name for a crocodile, or write a poem on a black beetle.

When a man falls into the water, to know how to swim will be of more use to him than all his mathematics, and yet how very few boys learn swimming! Girls are taught dancing and French when stitching and English would be of hundred per cent more use to them. When men have to earn their livings, in these hard times, a good trade and industrious habits will serve their turn a world better than all the classics. Who nowadays advocates practical training at our schools? Schoolmasters would go into spasms if they were asked to teach poor people's boys to hoe potatoes and plant cauliflowers, and yet school boards would be doing a power of good if they did something of the sort. If you want a dog to be a pointer or a setter, you train him accordingly: why ever don't they do the same with men? It ought to be "every man for his business, and every man master of his busi-

VERY IGNORANT PEOPLE

ness." Let Jack and Tom learn geography by all means, but do not forget to teach them how to black their own shoes, and put a button on to their own trousers. As for Jane and Sally, let them sing and play the music if they like, but not till they can darn a stocking and make a shirt. When they mend the education act I hope they will put in a clause to teach children practical commonsense home duties as well as the three R's. What's the use of talking this way, for if children are to learn common sense where are we to get the teachers? Very few people have any of it to spare, and those who have are never likely to take to school keeping. Lots of girls learn nothing except what I think they call "accomplishments." There's poor man with six girls, and little a year to keep his family on, and yet not one of them can do a hand's turn. Their mother would go into spasms lest Miss Sophia should have chapped hands through washing the family linen, or lest Alexandra should spoil her complexion in picking a few gooseberries for a pudding. It is enough to make a cat laugh to hear the poor things talk about fashion and etiquette when they are not half as well off as the daughters down the street, who earn their own living, and are laying money by against the time of need. Trust me, he who marries these highty-tighty young ladies will have as bad a bargain as if he married a wax doll. How the fat would be in the fire if Mrs. Gent heard me say it, but I do say it for all that—she and her girls are *ignorant, very ignorant,* because they do not know what would be of most service to them.

Every sprat nowadays calls itself a herring; every donkey thinks itself fit to be one of the Queen's horses; every candle reckons itself the sun. But when a man with his best coat on, and a paper collar, a brass chain on his waistcoat, a cane in his hand, and emptiness in his head, fancies that people cannot see through his swaggers and brags, he must be *ignorant, very ignorant,* for he does not know himself. Flats, dressed up to the top of the fashion, think themselves somebodies, but nobody else does. Dancingmasters and tailors may rig up a fop, but they cannot make a nothing into a man. You may color a millstone as much as you like, but you cannot make it into a cheese.

Round our part we have a lot of poets, at least a set of *very ignorant* people who think they are; and these folks worry me more than a little because I have written a book, and therefore ought to listen to their rigmaroles. Nonsense is nonsense whether it rhymes or not, just as bad money is good for nothing whether they jingle or lie quiet. "Here, John," said a man to me, "I want to read you some of my verses." "No, thank you," said I, "I don't feel in a poetical frame of mind today." What right has that fellow to shoot his rubbish at my door? I have enough of my own. I do not intend to have my ear stuffed up with cobbler's wax or cobbled verses. I had a double dose the other morning from two of our great village poets, and I must confess it was rather better than most of the rhymes that I meet with in books. Chubbins said,

"It is a sin to steal a pin,"

And then Padley topped it up by adding,

"It is a greater to steal a tater."

When people lend money at outrageous interest and think to make their fortunes by it, they must be *ignorant, very ignorant*. As well hang a wooden kettle over the fire to boil the water for tea, or sow beans in a river and look for a fine crop.

When men believe in lawyers and lenders (whether Jews or Gentiles), and borrow money, and speculate, and think themselves lucky fellows, they are shamefully ignorant. The very gander on the common would not make such a stupid of himself, for he knows when anyone tries to pluck him, and will not lose his feathers and pride himself in the operation.

The man who spends his money with the publican, and thinks that the landlord's bows and "How do ye do, my good fellow?" mean true respect, is a perfect natural; for with them it is

> If you have money, take a seat;
> If you have none, take to your feet.

The fox admires the cheese; if it were not for that he would not care a rap for the raven. The bait is not put into the trap to feed the mouse, but to catch him. We do not light a fire for the herring's comfort, but to roast him for our own eating. If I spend money for the good of any house let it be my own and not the landlord's. It's a bad well into which you must put water; and the dramhouse is a bad friend, because it takes all, and leaves you nothing but heeltaps and headaches. He who calls those his friends who let him sit and drink by the hour, is *ignorant, very ignorant*. Why, Red Lions, and Tigers, and Eagles, and Vultures, are all creatures of prey, and none but fools put themselves within the power of their jaws and talons.

He who believes in promises made at elections has long ears, and may try to eat thistles. Mr. Plausible has been round asking all the working men for their votes, and he will do all sorts of good things for them. Will he? Yes, the day after tomorrow—a little later than never. Poor men who expect the "friends of the working man" to do anything for them, must be *ignorant, very ignorant*. When they get their seats, of course they cannot stand up for their principles except when it is to their own interest to do so.

To lend umbrellas and look to have them sent home, to do a man a good turn and expect another from him when you want it, to dream of stopping some women's tongues, to try to please everybody, to hope to hear gossips speak well of you, or to reckon upon getting the truth of a story from common report, are all evidences of great ignorance.

Those who know the world best trust it least: those who trust it at all are not wise; as well trust a horse's heel or a dog's tooth! Trusting to others ruins many. He who leaves his business to bailiffs and servants, and believes that it will be well done, must be *ignorant, very ignorant*. The mouse knows when the cat is out of the house, and servants know when the master is away. No sooner is the eye of the master gone than the hand of the workman slackens; at least, it is so nine times out of ten. "I'll go myself," and "I'll see to it," are two good servants on a farm. Those who lie in bed, and bolster themselves up with the notion that their trade will carry on itself, are *ignorant, very ignorant*.

Such as drink and live riotously, and wonder why their faces are so blotchy and their pockets so bare, would leave off wondering if they had two grains of wisdom. We might put all their wit in an eggshell, or they would never be such dupes as to hunt after comfort where it is no more to be found than a cow in a crow's nest. Alas! good-for-nothings are common as mice in a wheat-rick. I only wish we could pack them off to Lubberland, where they would be paid for sleeping. If some one could let loose fellows see the sure result of ill-living, perhaps they might reform. Yet, I don't know, for they do see it, and yet go on all the same; like a moth that burns its wings in the flame and yet dashes into the candle again. Cer-

VERY IGNORANT PEOPLE

tainly for loitering lushingtons to expect to thrive by keeping their hands in their pockets, or their noses in pewter mugs, proves them to be *ignorant, very ignorant*.

When I see a young lady with a flower garden on her roof, and a dress shop on her body, tossing her head about as if she thought everybody was charmed, I am sure she must be *ignorant, very ignorant*. Sensible men do not marry a wardrobe or a bonnet-box; they want a woman of sense, and women of that kind always dress sensibly, not gaudily.

To my mind, those who sneer at religion, and set themselves up to be too knowing to believe in the Bible, are shallow fellows. They generally use big words, and bluster a great deal, but if they fancy they can overturn the faith of thinking people, who have tried and proved the power of the grace of God, they must be *ignorant, very ignorant*. He who looks at the sunrise and the sunset, and does not see the footprints of God, must be inwardly blinder than a mole, and only fit to live underground. God seems to talk to me in every primrose and daisy, to smile upon me from every star, to whisper to me in every breath of morning air, and to call aloud to me in every storm. It is strange that so many educated gentlemen see God nowhere, while John the plowman feels him everywhere. John has no wish to change places, for the sense of God's presence is his comfort and joy. They say that man is the god of the dog: those men must be worse than dogs who will not listen to the voice of God, for a dog obeys its master's whistle. They call themselves "philosophers," do they not? Their proper name is fools, for the fool hath said in his heart, "There is no God." The sheep know when rain is coming, the swallows foresee the winter, and even the pigs, they say can see the wind; how much worse than a brute must he be who lives where God is everywhere present, and yet sees Him not! Thus it is very clear that a man may be a great hand at learning and yet be *ignorant, very ignorant.*